When You Kant
Figure It Out,
Ask a Philosopher

When You Kant Figure It Out, Ask a Philosopher

Timeless Wisdom for Modern Dilemmas

Marie Robert

Translated by Meg Richardson

Little, Brown Spark
New York Boston London

Little, Brown Spark
Hachette Book Group
1290 Avenue of the Americas, New York, NY 10104
littlebrownspark.com

First North American edition: November 2019
Originally published in France as *Kant tu ne sais plus quoi faire, il reste la philo* by Flammarion/Versilio: April 2018

Little, Brown Spark is an imprint of Little, Brown and Company, a division of Hachette Book Group, Inc. The Little, Brown Spark name and logo are trademarks of Hachette Book Group, Inc.

The publisher is not responsible for websites (or their content) that are not owned by the publisher.

The Hachette Speakers Bureau provides a wide range of authors for speaking events. To find out more, go to hachettespeakersbureau.com or call (866) 376-6591.

Illustrations by Paige Vickers

Book design by Marie Mundaca

ISBN 978-0-316-49252-2
LCCN 2019946525

10 9 8 7 6 5 4 3 2 1

LSC-C

Printed in the United States of America

To Buffignécourt, to the Petite Maison, to Rue Didot, and to their owners...

Contents

CONTENTS

CONTENTS

Preface

*F*our hours spent wandering the aisles of IKEA for nothing. All hope was lost. I was ready to slap the next person who uttered a cute Swedish word as I walked into yet another room full of boxes and began to cry.

The day had started so well. I'd had a plan: I had basically learned the entire IKEA catalogue by heart and made a careful list, all set to prove to the world just how type A and efficient I could be. But now, much like the spatula display I had just knocked over, my grand plan had come crashing down. Stumbling through the aisles of that huge store, surrounded by real adults who clearly had their lives together and their furniture in a cart, I felt even more helpless and pathetic by comparison. I was in meltdown mode: lost in IKEA and lost in life.

How could I make myself feel better? I considered stretching out on a bed named after a Viking, or stealing a bottle of vodka, but then I had a better idea: Baruch Spinoza. He's always been one of my favorite philosophers. I sat in a corner of the store and imagined my old friend Baruch handing me a cappuccino and comforting me. I pictured him reminding

3

me that desire is what makes us alive, what drives us to move forward in life—and I stopped crying. Suddenly IKEA, and my life, felt far less overwhelming. As I stood up and wiped my eyes, I realized that philosophy had saved my day.

In that corner of IKEA, the idea for this book was born. It's about twelve philosophers who can help us keep it together, even when everything in our lives seems to be falling apart. In the following chapters I will talk about life's chaotic, difficult times: when we're angry, embarrassed, scared, or confused. People have to find ways to get through these times day after day, year after year. What better way to deal with challenging moments than philosophy? Why not turn to the words and ideas that have been helping people make sense of their existence for centuries?

I want to get philosophy out of the library and into bars, dinner parties, offices, and people's everyday lives so it can be what it was meant to be: wisdom that helps us navigate life, not something pretentious and abstract. Studying philosophy should not mean reading something in a book and then forgetting about it. Philosophy should make our lives more meaningful. It should comfort and free us. It should help us cope with the difficult parts of our lives—whether we're getting ready for a date, arguing with a teenager, or grieving a dead pet.

Taking philosophy down from its pedestal is the best

thing we can do for it, and us. If we can get acquainted with these great thinkers, when the next moment of crisis arrives, instead of freaking out and crying in IKEA, we can sit down and have a coffee with Aristotle, Plato, or Kant and hash it all out until we feel better.

Spinoza Goes to IKEA

Or, the Problem with Desires

*I*t's 9:54 a.m. on a Saturday. You wake up filled with joy, knowing you have the next forty-eight hours all to yourself—two entire days to do whatever your heart desires. You'll catch up on your favorite Netflix shows, drink a leisurely coffee, have dinner with friends; you might even be good and go to the gym. You lie in bed for a few more moments until your gaze falls on your bookshelf. Yikes. Your little bookshelf is in big trouble: it's sagging in the middle.

It's an important bookshelf, full of your most treasured possessions: the twelve books on meditation you bought last year, your high school yearbooks, the souvenirs you got on that trip to India in your twenties, and the encyclopedias you will never get rid of, no matter how much faster the internet is.

You could do some decluttering, but everything on that

shelf is really special to you. You couldn't bear to part with any of it. You decide it would be better to buy a second bookshelf—then you'll have more space for your mementos and knickknacks. You leap out of bed and call your boyfriend. You convince him to get brunch and do a little shopping with you at the playground for adults that is IKEA. I-K-E-A. Those four yellow letters are so familiar and comforting; they have accompanied you since you moved into your first apartment in college. You love everything about IKEA furniture—the slabs of wood, the instruction booklets, the adorable and unpronounceable names, the charming Swedish-ness of it all.

The car is ready: the trunk empty so it can be filled with IKEA treasures. You realize you could also probably do with some new saucepans and bedsheets, and maybe a new TV stand, and actually a cute coffee table would really spruce up the living room. You clutch the dog-eared IKEA catalogue like a treasure map.

You pull into the parking lot and drag your boyfriend toward the big blue box. This is what dreams are made of. The adventure begins. It's a pretty easy adventure, compared to, say, rock climbing or skydiving—all you have to do is follow the little arrows on the floor. IKEA is in control, leading you down this path, and you are loving it. You round the first bend and grab an extra catalogue with childlike glee. You gaze at the model apartments, all there to show that true happiness comes from buying sleek storage containers.

You're hungry for more. You see the bedroom section in the distance, with a sign above it that reads like something a family therapist might say: SEPARATE WITHOUT DIVIDING. By the time you get to the kids' section, your legs are starting to get sore. You've been wandering around for two hours already and your basket is basically empty, except for a tartan rug, three packets of paper napkins with reindeer on them, and two plastic ladles, which will come in handy if you ever decide to go on one of those soup-based diets. You are tired, but you feel alive. An instinct deep within you propels you around the store and whispers, *Spend more money!*

You try to pick up the pace, but then you see the cutest little stuffed crocodiles and you have to stop. Your boyfriend rolls his eyes and says, "So, is this guy going to end up like the kangaroo from last year, covered in dust at the back of the closet?" Clearly he doesn't understand how important this is to you, so you run over his toes with your cart and pretend not to hear him yelp. With a burst of newfound energy generated by a combination of sweat and frustration, you veer away from the arrows and chart your own course. You cut the wrong way across the office supply section, knocking over a fancy swivel chair that gets in your way. You make it to the lighting aisle, where you gnaw on the end of your mini pencil in an attempt to calm down, but it's no use. Now you're among the storage containers, you've lost sight of familiar landmarks, and your trusty catalogue was left behind on a pile of napkin holders. You're enraged. You start grabbing things left, right, and center. Nothing can stop you. When your boyfriend asks how you plan to get all this stuff home, you point a screw gun at him. What is happening to you? You've turned into a monster. You know you should try to control yourself, but this feeling cannot be tamed. On most days you can wax lyrical about the dangers of consumerism, but not today. Right now you have an insatiable need to buy stuff.

This day has turned into a disaster. The coffee table in the catalogue has misled you—the measurements are all wrong. You hear someone yell at the other end of the aisle, "Why didn't you measure first?" The TV stand that looked so classy in the catalogue looks cheap and plywood-y in real life. And you recognize the funky coatrack from the last Airbnb you stayed in, and you hate giving in to conformity. You can't slow down now. You grab four cranberry-vanilla candles, two packets of plates, and a plastic yucca plant, which you hide in your yellow cart. You can't control yourself. Your boyfriend stares at you like you're crazy. You glare back at him as he breaks a halogen lightbulb by throwing it into the cart. By the time you approach the self-service checkout, things are reaching the boiling point. Your boyfriend won't stop telling you he doesn't want to spend the next month messing around with a screwdriver every night. The rest of your desired items are waiting for you to find them somewhere between aisles B18 and D24, according to the reference numbers you carefully noted on your phone. Finally you can see light at the end of the tunnel.

But then, to your horror, you realize that your phone is dead. You have to either walk down every aisle again or kiss all of your precious furniture goodbye. If you leave now, your thirst will never be quenched. You. Must. Keep. Going.

The next part is a blur. There are tears, insults, despair, and then a receipt for $278.68 and a cart full of completely useless objects. You get into your car. You are fuming and your relationship is a wreck, all because you wanted to buy some stupid shelves. It's 7:14 p.m. The traffic on the way home gives you plenty of time to reflect on your sore muscles, your sweat-drenched clothes, your despair, and your hatred of blue and yellow.

What Would Spinoza Have to Say About All of This?

It's important to say, off the bat, that Spinoza wouldn't have been caught dead in IKEA. But Spinoza—or Baruch, if you're on first-name terms—had some thoughts about desire, virtue, and adversity that are going to help you out of your post-IKEA funk.

First of all, Spinoza can help you understand how your humanity works so you can better understand your actions. He had a very comforting theory that every individual is characterized by a "conatus," which sounds like an unfortunate condition but is basically just an urge or a drive—the thing that gets you out of bed in the morning and makes you appreciate life's pleasures.

Okay, let's back up for a second. According to Spinoza, people are part of nature, which is made by God. We are all created by the divine, meaning we all contain an energy that came straight from heaven, and we work hard to protect that energy. The conatus is our protected zone; we're ready to do just about anything to keep it intact. It's what makes us natural beings and not video game characters. This conatus has another name, which is less fun to say but maybe easier to understand: desire. This is where Spinoza becomes a great therapist. If he'd had a podcast, it would've been the perfect thing to listen to during an afternoon of shopping. Spinoza's philosophy is that your desires, wishes, and passions drive you and make you who you are. It's pointless to fight these forces. It's impossible to separate yourself from them, because they are your very essence. You shouldn't think of desire as something negative. Having desire is good! It means you're in the VIP section of all organic life forms. Spinoza wrote that "desire is the essence of man," and we'll include women in that too.

It's impossible to let go of desire, or to constrain and manage it, because the conatus is all-powerful. Bad credit is no match for a person's conatus. Neither is an apartment overflowing with IKEA furniture. The only thing that can stop it? Death. Desire will be with you for every step of your life. But you don't just wake up in the morning full of desire. It doesn't exist in the abstract, blowing around in the wind. In fact, desire reveals itself through certain situations—when you're at IKEA daydreaming in front of a giant pile of paper napkins, for example. Desire is only activated in certain contexts, but once it's active, it sets your thoughts alight.

So, according to Spinoza's ideas about morality, if you feel like your desires are dragging you down and changing every week—desires for fancy coffees, vacations, first dates, activities, or objects—don't worry. You're not going crazy. You just have a very healthy amount of Spinozan conatus.

You're a human being, and it's normal and good that your desires make themselves known. Your desires keep you on your toes and mean that you're a part of nature. Just by analyzing people's desires, Spinoza made the point that to desire isn't something negative. There is no need to punish yourself for having desires; in fact, it's actually beneficial to human existence that you have them.

And that's not all. Good old Baruch's advice about virtue can help calm you down too. For Spinoza, being virtuous doesn't mean going on a new juice cleanse every week, or restraining yourself when you want to roll your eyes at your annoying coworkers, or stopping yourself from dancing in public when your favorite Beyoncé song comes on. And it certainly doesn't mean you have to stop going to a certain big blue Swedish establishment. Virtue is about trying to understand your passions—figuring out what drives you and makes you happy. Listening to your deepest self is the best hope you have of finding the satisfaction and peace everyone is searching for. The wisest people are not necessarily the most disciplined and reasonable. They are the people who can come to a true understanding of the world around them, and an understanding of what parts of that world drag them down instead of lift them up. As Marie Kondo would say, it's all about knowing what sparks joy—not about cutting out desire entirely! Having desire is normal and healthy. It's important to recognize desire for what it is, so you don't get frustrated with yourself when it shows up. Being virtuous doesn't mean putting a muzzle on your conatus; it means getting to know your conatus and becoming comfortable with it.

So, think of Spinoza the next time you go to IKEA. Pat yourself on the back for being so full of desire. But also, take a few minutes to listen to your heart and ask yourself if you really, deeply desire all the things in your cart. If you can think like this, the next time you pull out of the IKEA parking lot, your heart—and shopping bags—will be much lighter.

Spinoza at a Glance (1632–1677)

Born on November 24, 1632, in Amsterdam, Baruch Spinoza lived an eventful life. In 1656, he was kicked out of the Jewish community for expressing anti-religious ideas and had to move far away from his family. Spinoza's book *The Ethics* was a huge bestseller when it came out after his death in 1677. He wanted to come up with a practical philosophy that would help people feel free and at peace. He paved the way for nerds with expensive tastes for years to come, asking questions like: "How should we deal with desires that get in the way of our lives and our relationships with others?" "Which passions and desires are productive and reaffirm who we are?" "How can we break away from passivity and become active?" He explores all of these questions, with added thoughts about God, nature, and even geometry.

The Book You Need in a Crisis: The Ethics

To put your life and mind in order, look no further than *The Ethics*. In this radical book, published posthumously to avoid censorship, Spinoza developed his thoughts mathematically, resulting in a step-by-step guide to God, liberty, and passion.

Philosophy to the Rescue

- Your desires prove that you're human. Desires are a reminder of the miraculous force within you that makes you want to get up in the morning.
- You shouldn't fight your desires. They're irrepressible and infinite. It's better to recognize and work with your desires than to feel guilty about them.
- Wisdom comes from understanding yourself. You shouldn't beat yourself up about your desires. You should just try to understand who you are and where you're going. Learn to listen to yourself.

Aristotle and Hangovers

Or, Believing in the Experience

*T*his time it's for real. You've sworn on every holy book you can think of—you will never wake up with a hangover again. You're done feeling like your skull is a soccer stadium at the end of the World Cup final. You're done waking up with stinging eyes, a spinning head, and an upset stomach. To your friends, you've become that sitcom character who at some point in the evening says, "Guyyss. I'm going to remember this night foreverrrr!" as you stumble around, unable to keep your balance, spilling your drink on everyone around you.

Let's be honest: you've sacrificed your body and soul to the gods of debauchery for a long time. And that's nothing to be ashamed of. Your partying résumé is impressive—you've been working on it for years. Your weekend nights usually begin with a frantic exchange of text messages while you and your friends decide where to meet. Then you head out into the night with a nonchalant look you've perfected over the years. You're ready for anything. You make small talk with your friends over a drink at the bar, before you really get into it and your dignity starts disappearing quicker than the ice cubes in your mojitos. The music is pumping—you throw your hands into the air and scream the lyrics to whatever song is playing.

Sweat clings to everything, bass rattles the glasses on the bar, strobe lights flash—you're on fire. It doesn't matter that you're wasted; you're having a blast. You're a firm believer that alcohol-induced swaying around or even falling on the floor counts as dancing.

As a new day dawns, you set off on a quest for a burger. You're so ravenous you'd chase down an animal and make it into a burger yourself if you had to. But instead, you find a burger place that's open late, or early, and you sit there trying to piece together your memories from the night before, editing out the embarrassing parts.

Your weekends are roller coasters. You feel young and invincible one minute, then guilty for living like this the next, until finally, one day you decide it needs to stop. You've had your fun, but it's time to turn over a new leaf. It's time to listen to your body, and your body is telling you it would rather be perfecting yoga poses than dancing, half dressed, on a table.

Armed with a long list of resolutions, you're basically a health guru now. You tell anyone who will listen about how much you love being gluten-free. You love it as much as you used to love being decadent. You don't drink cocktails anymore, no, no. Now you drink green juice every morning at 6:00 a.m., after you've meditated and before you go running. You're proud of this journey you're taking, this process of self-discovery. You're living off essential oils and love alone. Gone are the Sunday afternoons when you would lie in front of the TV feeling hungover and sorry for yourself. You're a new person now.

When you get an invitation to "the craziest party of the year," you smile a saintly smile. It's like the universe is testing you. You have to prove how evolved you are, and that you can resist temptation, even when it's hard. You'll go to this party and show your friends that you can be responsible. You say the word to yourself, drawing it out so it's as long as the list of foods you don't eat anymore. You text people before just to let them know that you'll have to leave by midnight. You'll spend the night making good choices and being nice to everyone. Basically, you're the most mature, put-together person who ever lived.

When you walk into the bar, you ooze confidence and you feel slightly superior to everyone else. They can't resist temptations, but you can. It's good to watch the party from a distance, knowing that you're doing what's best for your well-being. At 11:00 p.m., you still feel great. You tell everybody about your new diet. At 11:30 p.m., you're getting your stuff from the coat check when you run into an old friend. She wants you to stay for one last drink in honor of "the good old days." After a bit of negotiation with your mind, body, and soul, you decide that one gin and tonic won't do any harm.

But at 1:00 a.m., you're squashed into a taxi with five other people, heading to a club you can't remember the name of. You tell yourself that sweating a bit will help with the detox you're doing that week. By 3:00 a.m., you're climbing onto a table and singing along to the hit of the summer at the top of your lungs. At 4:00 a.m., you can barely remember your address. At 5:00 a.m., your resolutions are history.

What goes up must come down. What starts as a crazy Saturday night ends as a miserable Sunday afternoon. It's 2:02 p.m. and there you are. Your head is spinning and your legs are sore from dancing. You've broken all of your promises to yourself and you feel horrible. What happened to being responsible? You're exhausted and full of guilt. You would give anything to take it all back. You should have stayed home and watched a documentary like a real adult.

What Would Aristotle Have to Say About All of This?

There's no historical evidence that Aristotle liked to party, but he had a lot to say about self-esteem and how to live. In his book *Nicomachean Ethics,* one of the most famous works of ancient philosophy, Aristotle tried to answer the question "What is the best way for humans to act?" He didn't want his work to be philosophy for the sake of philosophy. He wanted his ideas about virtue and ethics to have practical applications and results in the real world. He wanted to figure out what humans should be striving for. After he defined what he saw as an ideal way to exist, he laid out some guidelines for how to exist in that way.

Though a drunken Saturday night might not seem like a worthy end in itself by Aristotle's standards, he would still want you to think of the night as an experience to draw wisdom from. He said that every moment in your life, even the disappointing or embarrassing ones, can be used to gain a deeper understanding of yourself. That's a pretty comforting thought. It's no wonder Aristotle's ideas have survived for 2,500 years of humans making mistakes and feeling guilty.

Aristotle answered the questions "What should influence our actions?," "What should we strive for?," and other such dilemmas with one word: "goodness." Don't panic.

Goodness isn't some lofty thing that is almost impossible to achieve. For Aristotle, goodness is basically synonymous with happiness. The goal of thinking about morality and ethics is to help people feel more in harmony with themselves. Being virtuous doesn't mean depriving yourself of a fun night out with friends. Being virtuous is more about giving yourself the possibility of being happy. In everyday language, being "virtuous" can mean being a bit uptight, but the way Aristotle sees it, being virtuous just means learning to live well and be happy.

However, it gets a little more complicated. For Aristotle, happiness is not related to physical pleasure or to social interactions. He talked about a meditative, wise kind of happiness that comes when you're able to find courage, balance, and serenity in life. Aristotle said that deep, true happiness isn't contingent upon the outside world; it comes from within. And he offered advice on how to find it.

As you start out on this journey to Aristotelian happiness, you have to be patient. Arriving at real happiness takes some work. To find true happiness, you have to be virtuous, but you can't just become virtuous overnight. Virtue comes from living and gaining Experience. Experience with a capital *E* is made up of lots of tiny day-to-day experiences. This is the key. It is only by living, wading through the good and the bad, that you will make progress in your quest to understand the world and yourself, and learn to listen to your reason.

So, a Sunday hangover has its benefits; it can teach you something. Dealing with this hangover is one of many steps on a journey to truly feeling good and living well. If you learn from this experience, the next time you go out you will remind yourself that after two cocktails it's probably time to go to bed or stop drinking. To take full advantage of these kinds of experiences, you must listen to yourself, prove that you can be patient, and celebrate your day-to-day victories.

You have to understand that living virtuously can and should be something constant. Feeling guilty doesn't make you a better person, but the experience you gain from living through your misadventures does. Making resolutions and putting restrictions on yourself will not make you into a perfect person living a perfect life. Life will never stop throwing experiences at you. You will never arrive at a static, perfect state of being. But by pushing through experience after experience, you will start to reshape your life. The goal is not to be perfect or to stop making mistakes entirely. The goal is to not make the same mistake over and over again, and to always be evolving.

According to Aristotle, virtue lies somewhere between knowledge and action. To make progress, you have to take action: you have to keep moving through life, challenging your old beliefs, and trying new things, even if that means making mistakes.

The aim is to be able to make the right choices again and again so they become ordinary. Aristotle famously said, "We are what we repeatedly do. Excellence, then, is not an act but a habit." The next time you get invited to a party, don't stay at home in bed, but also don't go to the party and make the same mistakes you've made dozens of times before. Say no to that gin and tonic and take care of yourself, knowing you'll be rewarded for your virtuous decisions with a blissful, hangover-free Sunday morning.

Aristotle at a Glance (384–322 BCE)

Aristotle was born in 384 BCE on an island in the Cyclades. He started his philosophical training at age seventeen when he joined Plato's Academy. There, he sharpened his mind surrounded by the greatest Greek thinkers of his time. Aristotle was Alexander the Great's private tutor until he opened his own school, called the Lyceum. He liked to reflect on life while going on walks with his students, so that his mind would stay in motion just like his body. A jack-of-all-trades when it came to philosophy, he pondered a lot of different subjects across disciplines, like ethics, logic, politics, medicine, and physics. He even laid the foundations for the ways in which we think about many of these subjects today. He's been translated and interpreted in Christian and Muslim traditions, and remains one of the most widely studied philosophical thinkers in the world.

The Book You Need in a Crisis:
Nicomachean Ethics

If your dad dedicated a book to you about being good, it could be the greatest compliment...or passive-aggressiveness at its finest. Dedicated to (or edited by) Aristotle's son Nicomachus, *Nicomachean Ethics* gets at the heart of what the highest form of goodness is. Turns out, happiness has a lot to do with it—but Aristotle shows that people often disagree about how to be happy. The quest continues!

Philosophy to the Rescue

- The goal of existing is to be happy. Happiness can come from different sources: pleasure, honor, glory, etc. But the greatest happiness is one that depends on you alone, and not on the outside world.
- To attain happiness, you have to be virtuous. That doesn't mean you can never go to another club, just that you should find a balance that works for you. This takes time, but it's always worth it.
- The most important piece of the happiness puzzle is experience, something you are constantly constructing.

Only by living, taking action, and making mistakes will you discover yourself and put your reason to good use. As Aristotle rightly said, "Knowing yourself is the beginning of all wisdom."

Nietzsche: Just Do It

Or, Winning the Race Against Yourself

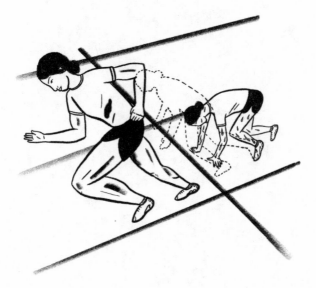

*Y*ou've imagined the finish line millions of times. You have the whole movie in your head. You can almost feel your burning muscles, your aching joints, the single drop of sweat running down your forehead, the determined look in your eyes as you run toward the horizon. You put one foot in front of the other. It's an out-of-body experience. You can't feel pain. Then finally there it is: the finish line. You fall to your knees. The crowd goes wild. The chorus of "We Are the Champions" booms in time to your heartbeat. It's glorious. You give your teammates an emotional hug. They and everyone else are in awe of you. When you play the movie in your head, it usually ends with a shot of you being interviewed, glowing with the modesty of a hero who is accustomed to the taste of victory.

You love replaying this dream of being a champion athlete.

You've basically been thinking about it since you learned to walk. You've gotten sponsors, you've broken records, you're a legend...but only in your dreams.

Then one day you decide to turn your dream into a reality. You're going to run your very first marathon. You fill out the registration forms, feeling like you've overcome fear and laziness. You're just one pair of shoes away from running down your dream.

You're invigorated and ready to start doing hill sprints, intervals, and long runs—that's runner lingo. You decide on a nine-month training plan and subscribe to *Runner's World*. You follow running pages on Facebook and debate the merits of different energy gels in the comment sections of running blogs. You compare different types of shoe inserts and spend multiple Saturdays at the running store, learning to understand the subtleties of your stride. The salesperson is an expert on fragile tendons. You want to be the best. You have an iron will. You've stopped going out and partying. You're racking up sacrifices for this dream.

After a few months, you feel a sense of pride that you've never felt before. You know all of your hard work is going to pay off. Your thighs and your ego are swelling. Every time you do a long run, your confidence grows. You're free from self-doubt. The world is your racecourse. Your mind, body, and spirit are getting stronger. You feel an uncontrollable urge to run every morning—an urge to push your limits. You chant to yourself, "I run, therefore I am." You look at the numbers on your fancy new Fitbit and your Garmin, and you feel a distinct sense of satisfaction.

Finally, nine months have passed and you're ready to become the champion marathon runner you've always been in your dreams. The course is set up. You've tied and untied your shoelaces five times so they're not too loose and not too tight. You've spent hours perfecting your motivational playlist. But as you're warming up, your feet start to feel heavy and your back begins to ache. You see yourself in a store window as you stride by and you look stupid—nothing like the muscly Greek warrior you imagine yourself to be. No amount of menthol cream or ibuprofen can save you. You get vertigo when you look down at your shoelaces. You're no longer the lead in an inspirational action movie; you're more like a bit-part actor in a TV medical series. You click through online forums on your phone, wondering what could possibly be causing this terrible feeling. Then you realize that you're suffering from something that no amount of physical training or fancy gels and creams can cure. You're nervous and panicking. You feel weak and like an impostor. You'll never make it to the finish line. You try to gather your thoughts. You can't just let this dream evaporate. You need to get back in touch with your inner champion. You're going to need some coaching from a philosopher.

What Would Nietzsche Have to Say About All of This?

Friedrich Nietzsche was a sickly guy—definitely not an athlete, and not someone we would usually associate with sports. However, he has more advice to help athletes in his books than he has consonants in his name.

In order to get some motivation from Coach Nietzsche, let's take a quick detour and learn about the history of his ideas. It all started with Nietzsche's critique of Christianity. As Nietzsche saw it, religion—specifically prayer—makes people think of their lives on Earth as inconsequential in comparison to what happens in heaven. People can be so focused on praying and looking to God for meaning that they stop giving any thought to their everyday lives on Earth. But as Christianity loses ground in the modern world, people are no longer focusing on God the way they used to. Nietzsche went so far as to declare, "God is dead." This doesn't mean that people have stopped believing in God. It means that when most people make a decision, they no longer look toward their faith or a set of moral principles connected to religion.

Our old faith and our old set of morals were limiting but comforting. In today's world, as religion becomes less central to our lives, we have to come up with new morals, which isn't easy. A lot of the ideas our society was founded upon are not relevant anymore, and that creates problems.

Losing a moral structure results in nihilism, or the belief that life is meaningless. People often think of nihilism as a bad thing—a synonym for destruction. But according to Nietzsche, nihilism is much more complicated. Nietzsche described two forms of nihilism. First, there's passive nihilism. A passive nihilist says, "Why bother? What's the point?" A passive nihilist thinks humans can never really believe in anything, so it's not even worth trying to put together a structure of morals. This is the kind of thinking that makes people want to sit around and do nothing. It can make people lose any sense of themselves or their purpose. Understandably, passive nihilism can be viewed as something negative.

However, in *Thus Spoke Zarathustra,* Nietzsche countered this with the idea of active nihilism: because God is dead and we have lost our old values, we need to replace them with new values. As we construct new values, we need to remember the importance of ourselves as human beings on Earth. For too long when we've thought about morals, we've disregarded the fact that we are living, breathing earthly beings, because we have been so focused on religion. So, what better way to keep ourselves rooted in our existence on Earth than with physical challenges?

Nietzsche believed that every person has an inner energy. This energy acts as a motor and pushes the individual to keep going further and further. Nietzsche called this energy the "will to power." He wrote, "In my eyes, life is the instinct to believe, to last. Life is the accumulation of force, of power: where there is a deficit of drive and passion, there is decline." It is exactly this kind of power that we express when we practice a sport. Exercise triggers active nihilism. It is thanks to this power that humans will be able to build a new system of values and morals.

When you get stressed before a competition or an exam, you're often tempted to back off and hide from the challenge ahead. This is an example of passive nihilism—the feeling of detachment and hopelessness that makes you want to stay home, away from anything meaningful. Facing a challenge head-on is a way to remind yourself of your inner power, to remind yourself that you are alive.

Nietzsche also said that you need to not only keep your motor running but also challenge it so it develops and grows stronger. By constantly training this inner energy, you can reach what Nietzsche called a superhuman state. For Nietzsche, a superhuman isn't a perfect person or a person with amazing genes. A superhuman is an ideal to aim for—the strongest and best form of a human. By striving to be a superhuman, you push yourself further than you knew was possible. When you work to overcome your fears, when you push yourself past your comfort zone and out of your habits, you liberate the power inside yourself. By constantly growing your internal energy, you can keep finding new sources of joy in your life and be free to celebrate things that are truly important and useful—like pleasure, hard work, courage, and strength. These values don't come from God but from us, humans. We should celebrate the collapse of our old morals because we have the incredible opportunity to rebuild them. We have to use our active nihilism and let go of laziness, indifference, and passive nihilism in order to win at life.

As you wait on the marathon starting line and passive nihilism tries to knock you down, don't let it. You're stronger than that. You've made it to the starting line; the hardest part is over. Now it's time to make your dream come true. Play that movie in your head one more time and then go—become the superhuman you have always wanted to be.

Nietzsche at a Glance (1844–1900)

Friedrich Nietzsche was born in 1844 in Röcken, Prussia. He was a brilliant child, but he was tormented by existential anxiety. He wanted to learn everything. He loved poetry. He studied at the best schools, then became a philology professor at the University of Basel at the age of twenty-four. There he engrossed himself in ancient texts and analyzed them in detail. He was passionate about the ancient Greek thinkers and saw many ways to apply their ideas to his time. He was obsessed with creating a modern, German version of what he read from ancient Greece. He published numerous works that harshly criticized Christianity and classical morality because he saw both of them as putting too many constraints on life. In the last ten years of his life, he became very sick, dealing with fits of dementia and growing as weak as his philosophical ideas were strong.

The Book You Need in a Crisis: _Thus Spoke Zarathustra_

In this book, poet and prophet Zarathustra decides to shake things up a little, so he leaves his monotonous existence and gets lost in the mountains. Then he returns home to encourage people to reject the dull aspects of their lives that they have been tolerating. _Thus Spoke Zarathustra_ shows that when you try to follow a strict set of preexisting morals, you often paralyze your desire, your joy, and your creativity. Instead, you should listen to and understand your instincts—and then you'll be on your way to becoming Übermensch, or the most awesome human you can be.

Philosophy to the Rescue

- Rather than try to live your life within the constraints of somebody else's set of morals, it's important to think about your own personal morals and listen to your instincts.
- Every individual has an internal energy that needs to be challenged in order for that individual to grow.
- Being a superhuman isn't about checking off items on a list written by someone else. It's about learning to set your own personal goals and pushing yourself to be the person you really want to be.

No News Alerts Allowed in the Garden of Epicurus

Or, the Ethics of Mindfulness

What better way to relax after a rough week at work than a getaway with your friends. It's Friday night and your car is snuggled up in a traffic jam. The melodious sounds of honking horns and shouting fill the air. The fragrance of someone else's exhaust wafts into your car. (You're trying to use relaxing words to describe the situation so you can get a head start on your vacation mindset.) You're so ready for this weekend. You can't wait to sit in striped deck chairs and read inspiring books. Your schedule will be as flexible as a yogi. Dinners will be delicious and the conversations fulfilling. You're ready to be transported to another world, far away from your office, your grocery store, your problems—a perfect world where you will finally get to wind down.

You've been in dire need of a break for months, and now, as you inch through this traffic jam, you feel a sense of inner peace. You love the world around you. You love the road signs. You even love the bugs on your windshield. You turn off the radio. You'd rather listen to your happy thoughts than the sound of traffic updates.

Later, with your heart as full as your suitcase, you arrive at the charming house where you'll spend this glorious weekend. You're exhausted, and you can't wait to sink into bed and start becoming the best, most relaxed version of yourself you've ever been. You're going to appreciate every leaf on every tree and every breath of sea breeze you inhale. Nothing is going to get to you this weekend.

The next morning, you leap out of bed. You can't wait to say good morning to your friends. You join the breakfast table with a radiant smile, which quickly dulls. Your friends look like they're still half asleep, and they barely greet you. Their sagging eyes are glued to their phones. They sip their coffee morosely and mutter as they scroll through the latest news stories. It's like their phones are the real guests here: every thought, every sentence, passes through them; everything either comes from or ends up on Facebook, Twitter, Instagram, like the sites are part of your friends' DNA now. Before you've finished what you had hoped would be a lovely, relaxing cup of tea, you've already had to listen to your friends discuss two plane crashes, the fate of some poor dolphin who got washed up on a beach, half a dozen political scandals, and a few financial disasters.

This is not how you had envisioned the start of the day, and your soul is feeling just a little bit crushed, but you try to stay upbeat. These are people you care about, and even if you're bothered by their obsession with their phones and notifications, you're not going to let it get you down.

As the group is making lunch, things take a turn for the worse. Your childhood friend decides it would be nice to list every possible way the ingredients in the mixed salad will shave years off your life. He backs up his reasoning with testimonials from the internet and names of chemical compounds. As he's detailing all of the horrible things cucumbers can do to you, you start to see the harmless-looking salad as some kind of serial killer.

The conversation continues during lunch as you chew and swallow the deadly mixed salad. You feel nauseated. You try to tell yourself that it's all in your head, that your friend is just paranoid. You understand that we fear the world around us the way our ancestors once feared their gods, that anything can become scary if we want it to, but your appetite is completely gone.

Later, you go for a walk with another friend, thinking you'll finally be able to relax, but you've made the fatal mistake of forgetting that this friend is obsessed with conspiracy theories. And so as you try to take deep, rejuvenating breaths of the ocean air, he lays out all of the elaborate reasons why he is sure that aliens know the world's nuclear codes. You try to breathe even more deeply, but it's not working. You're definitely not relaxed. The salty spray from the sea and the sound of the crashing waves do nothing for you. The muscles in your neck tense up, and your head throbs. It's not the aliens' fault that you're feeling sick; it's your friends and their torrent of negativity.

While you're having cocktails that evening, you come to a terrible realization: your friends' phones are controlling them. They're chained to an endless stream of alerts and news flashes. The pretext is that they have to "stay up-to-date," but really, the screens are taking over, eating away at their souls. Society is in crisis, and it feels like you're power-less to do anything about it. As you and your friends clink your glasses, their phones ring and ding and buzz with more news they need to read and messages they need to answer. You know you should have empathy for them as they deal with this addiction, but they're completely ruining your weekend, and you don't know what to do.

For years now you've made it a habit not to look at newspaper headlines when you pass by newsstands. You've always preferred to look at some interesting architectural detail on an old building or a furniture store full of pretty lamps or frankly anything other than a bunch of headlines informing you of the terrible things happening in the world on any particular day. Nowadays, as headlines are more readily available on screens, you feel an even greater need to preserve your mental state. You hate screens, but they're everywhere. You can't take it anymore. There's a new tweet announcing the apocalypse every hour and a new envy-inducing Instagram post every minute. But these days, trying to avoid the notifications feels like walking on a tightrope in a windstorm.

Now, on this Saturday night with your friends that you've been looking forward to for months, you've fallen off your tightrope and you're swimming in a lake of bad news. You stay quiet. You want to tell your friends that you hate this conversation, but you don't know how. You don't want to come across as selfish or in denial, but this has to stop. You're starting to long for the traffic jam you were sitting in yesterday—the horns and the exhaust fumes and your cozy little car. Just sitting in that car would have made for a better vacation than this misery. If you don't come up with a way to get through the rest of the weekend, you're going to have to go hide in a closet until it's over.

What Would Epicurus Have to Say About All of This?

When you hear "Epicurus," you may think of the popular recipe website that bears a similar name. You may see the images flooding your inbox and newsfeed, of people in their fancy kitchens, whipping up gourmet food, drinking wine on gorgeous verandas, and loving life. Epicurus has come to be associated with a breezy, luxurious lifestyle. But actually, Epicurus's ideas about living life to the fullest have nothing to do with eating and drinking the latest cool thing that pops up on the internet. If you were to go to ancient Greece and visit Epicurus's garden, you would join his motley crew of followers and listen to him explain his ideas himself. He would not talk about the need to follow lifestyle blogs and to frantically stay up-to-date on the latest trends in what to eat and how to live. He would talk about a universal way to live well that worked in ancient Greece, and can still work today.

When he stretched out on his couch long ago, Epicurus didn't just think about concepts and come up with nice inspirational quotes. He thought about how to create a better way of life. It's important to remember that being a philosopher doesn't mean memorizing deep-sounding phrases so you can recite them at dinner parties and impress everyone. The Hellenists—and Epicurus in particular—saw philosophy as a way to help humankind advance and, most important, as a way to make us happier. According to Epicurus, being happy, above anything else, means being at peace. Being at peace means appreciating silence as well as time with friends. Being at peace means listening to your thoughts and celebrating nice weather and nature. Being at peace means not weighing down the spirit with pictures of disasters that might or might not be real and news flashes that do nothing but stress you out.

According to Epicurus, happiness comes to people who don't let other parts of their lives get in its way. Happiness, he said, is a union of two states: "aponia," the absence of pain in the body, and "ataraxia," the absence of fear and stress in the soul. If you can attain tranquility in both the body and the soul, aponia and ataraxia, then you can attain happiness.

When you're suffering from indigestion because you're worried about the salad you ate, and you're glancing up at the sky every few minutes to make sure you're not about to be bombed by aliens, it's hard to find any kind of tranquility. Aponia and ataraxia are the lovely couple everyone wants to go on vacation with. The only problem is that, like a lot of lovely couples, they can be hard to pin down.

Epicurus knew better than to guarantee a 100 percent success rate for his little "happiness program." He laid out a list of all of the things that can get in the way of the tranquility he thought so much about. He said that the one thing with the most power to ruin our days, our weekends, and our lives is fear. Fear comes in many different forms—fear of death, fear of what we can't control, fear of emotional suffering, and fear of never being happy. We're afraid to miss out on everything, whether it's a breaking news story or a photogenic restaurant that keeps popping up in our feed. We get stuck in a loop, trying to catch up on an endless stream of information—not because we want to but because we're afraid not to.

Clearly, 2,300 years after Epicurus was thinking about these different kinds of fears, not a whole lot has changed. We're still swimming in the same troubled waters, except now our anxieties get magnified by our constant access to media and other people's lives on our screens. So how do we keep from drowning? Epicurus will be our flotation device. He said that in order to stay sane, first we need to take time to reflect upon our fears, observe them, and understand where they're coming from. Then we need to sort them into fears caused by things we can do something about and fears caused by things we have no control over and need to accept.

There is no point in worrying about fate, because everything is governed by physics, which is completely out of our control. Worrying about death is pointless too. No matter what happens in our lives, we are going to die. We might as well just accept that and stop torturing ourselves. Also, there's no point in worrying about what will happen on Earth after we die, because obviously we won't be around. We fear emotional suffering, but we have to remember that it always goes away after a while, and even in the worst moments there is always something positive to focus on. That leaves the fear of not being happy, a fear that can be all-consuming. The only way to get over this fear is to become less dependent upon the exterior world, to be satisfied with the basics, and to let ourselves truly appreciate the joys of existing.

Epicurus's teachings encourage us to acknowledge every bit of happiness in our lives, to cherish the people and things we love, and to savor and take advantage of every possible opportunity to be happy—like the opportunity to spend two days in a house by the beach.

We should work to fulfill our most basic needs and wants, but we should also realize that most of what we think we need and want is superfluous. The process of sorting out which wants and needs are important is like the process of redecorating a house—when in doubt, go for what is simple and timeless. When we stop to think about it, our basic needs and wants are remarkably simple. Nobody needs a constant stream of headlines and notifications on their phone to survive or to be happy. If we can get back to focusing on what we truly need and want, the world inside our heads can become a more beautiful place—a world where aponia and ataraxia are in charge.

So back to the weekend with your friends. You need to explain some Epicurean philosophy to them. They think they're bettering themselves and the world by "staying informed"—reading about some heartbreaking, awful news story every second of every day. But really, they're putting themselves through a lot of misery for nothing. News media shows us an endless list of reasons to be worried and afraid. But at the end of the day, it's useless to spend all of our time tearing our hair out as we scroll through our phones. We have no control over most of what we read about in the news. We don't have the power to save every dolphin that washes up on a beach or to stop every airplane from crashing.

Being consumed by terrible news in the media does not make us more virtuous or altruistic. We're weighing ourselves down with problems we have no way to solve. Knowing about all of these problems does not make us better people. It makes us unable to be present in the moments we have been given on this Earth to live and to connect with others.

Knowing how to keep distressing information at a

distance, daring to walk away from conversations that are causing us pain, turning off the radio or the television, and setting down our phones and tablets gives us room to appreciate the privilege of being alive.

The next time you're having a drink with friends and they start talking about how the world is going to end, don't just smile and nod. Take a page out of Epicurus's book. Instead of running away and hiding in a corner, listen to what your friends have to say, but then ask them to remember what keeps their lives fulfilling and joyful, and have a conversation about that instead.

Epicurus at a Glance (342-270 BCE)

Epicurus was born on the island of Samos in 342 BCE. As a rebellious teenager, he began coming up with his own philosophies after he disagreed with a teacher's answers to his questions about chaos. He led a frugal life, studied philosophy, and was obsessed with consuming only what was absolutely necessary. Clearly our modern image of Epicurus as a symbol of living luxuriously has missed what he was really about. At thirty-five, he moved to Athens and bought a garden, which he turned into a school. He was a renowned and beloved teacher. He taught physics and believed that everything on Earth is caused by the movement of atoms, and that nothing is determined by gods. We know he was a prolific author and probably produced close to three hundred works, but only a few fragments of his letters have survived. We also know that his philosophies revolved around the ideas that tranquility is the key to a happy life and that we need to reduce our fears however we can. His ideas have withstood the test of time and have had a significant influence on the philosophers who came after him.

The Book You Need in a Crisis: <u>Letter to Menoeceus</u>

Have no fear, Epicurus is here. Epicurus's practical guide to happiness in this letter to his young disciple Menoeceus is the most famous summary of his doctrine. In *Letter to Menoeceus,* he explains that fear of death is the biggest culprit behind evil, and he advises readers not to let it get the better of them. Though death claimed Epicurus eventually, his letter's wisdom rings eternal.

Philosophy to the Rescue

- Wisdom is not reserved for philosophers. You can be wise and mindful in your everyday life by cutting out the parts of your life that cause you stress and unhappiness.
- Fear is an obstacle to happiness, and your fears are often unfounded.
- Happiness can be found by focusing on life's simple pleasures and knowing how to rejoice in the fact that you exist.

A Blind Date with Plato

Or, Getting Sick of Feeling Lovesick

*Y*our thumping heart, the butterflies in your stomach, the way your mind wanders when you're sitting at the computer, the constant distraction, the sleepless nights, the incessant checking of your cell phone, just in case a text came in while you weren't looking—you suffer the same symptoms every time you start dating someone new. Still, your faith in love is strong. Your life is basically a romantic comedy, with a very indecisive screenwriter and without the happy ending...yet. According to some of your friends, you're a hopeless romantic. According to others, you're impossibly picky—because either you ask for too much or you offer too little, depending on who you ask. People say you're looking for a Prince Charming who doesn't exist, that you're living in a fantasy world, or that you spend too much time with your parents instead of going out into the world. You smile and nod, but you know they are wrong. When the perfect person comes along, you'll know it immediately, and all of the disappointment, the blind dates, and the swiping will have been worth it. You have no doubt that one day you'll find yourself face-to-face with the one you've been searching for, and that's your light at the end of the tunnel. You feel that possibility, that "What if...?" in every conversation, and it energizes you. Every time you meet someone, you want to learn everything you possibly can about them, to help you imagine what it would be like to spend the rest of your lives together.

That conviction is how you ended up on this date. The guy you'll be meeting is some friend of a friend's distant cousin, fished out of a pool of single men by your optimistic (or maybe pitying) friends. Of course you've planned it all out, down to the last detail. You've thought hard about your outfit and about potential discussion topics. You've practiced what to say, like you would before a job interview—an interview for your dream job, not just some unpaid internship. The whole setup makes you smile. You love the way these moments unfold, when two people first encounter each other, both energized by curiosity. You love the careful words, the calculated hand gestures, the little white lies. (You've told people you're basically an Olympic-caliber skier, but the truth is you're scared of going down the blue runs.)

You go over the whole plan in your mind. You think about the mechanisms of seduction. You want your date to look at you with the same wonder and amazement as a person about to open a present. You walk slowly toward the entrance, savoring the last few minutes before this mystery person becomes someone real, made of flesh, bone, and feelings.

And then, finally, there he is. You say hello, and he goes in for a kiss on the cheek. It's a little awkward—your cheek doesn't feel like your own for a moment. You both sit down, a little clumsily, and take turns laughing politely, like people on a talk show. You order the sexiest-sounding drink, even though you worry it will make you nauseated. You stammer something vague about the décor and the uniqueness of the walls, which are, unfortunately, just beige. Internally, you pray for the magic to kick in. You need some help from Cupid ASAP.

You tell yourself to stay calm. You try to focus on things you have in common with this person and reasons why he might make a good life partner. So far, you haven't gathered much evidence. You start paying close attention to every word he utters—but the danger of paying close attention is that you might hear something you don't like. Or a lot of things you don't like. You try to see the best in this guy, but it's painfully obvious that he's starting almost all of his sentences with "Well, actually," which is not cool. It's a verbal tic, and an extremely annoying, condescending one. You can't help but notice that he hasn't asked you a single question, which could be seen as a little self-centered. Still, you give him the benefit of the doubt. Maybe he's just shy. Sometimes great people give bad first impressions when they're nervous. But...after three hours, as you listen to this guy tell an extremely detailed and serious story about his recent boomerang-throwing championship, you can't take it anymore. You order another cocktail to give you the strength to make it through. You've done a heroic job of saying "Reaaally?" "That's awesome," and "Wow!" but you've had enough. Clearly you and this person have nothing in common. Your short-lived dreams of a romance with your friend's friend's distant cousin are dead. You don't want to share anything with this guy ever again—except maybe the cost of these drinks.

Though you ought to be used to disappointing dates by now, you're suddenly overwhelmed with exhaustion. You wonder if all this is really worth it. You're about ready to lay down your sword, or maybe use it to stab Aphrodite and Cupid and whoever else was supposed to help you out with this whole falling-in-love thing. Your friends were right all along. You've been acting ridiculous, drowning in childish fantasies about love. As you walk home, all roads point to the nunnery, but for some strange reason you feel a ray of optimism stirring within you—and it's not just the cocktails. How is it possible that after such a disastrous date, you're still holding out hope that the love of your life is waiting around the corner? Are you completely crazy to still believe in love? You need to call in some backup to reassure you.

What Would Plato Have to Say About All of This?

It's hard to believe that the namesake of "platonic love"—the non-romantic, non-sexual kind of love—can help you justify your beliefs about romance and your desire for a romantic partner. But Plato is going to give you some reasons why your quest for true love isn't as hopeless and silly as it might seem after a bad date.

Plato's book *Symposium* is set at a lively banquet where eight members of Greek high society have gathered. During the meal, they reflect upon love and lovers. The poet Aristophanes recounts a myth of a long-ago time when there were three types of human beings: men, women, and a third, genderless kind of being who was both male and female. All three genders were spherical beings, with four arms, four legs, and two sexual organs each, and they were all perfectly happy and complete.

The strange, spherical creatures felt like they had everything they could possibly need, but they were full of themselves. They decided to go to heaven, compete with the gods, and try to overthrow them. When Zeus saw the beings climbing up toward his kingdom, he flew into a rage. At first he wanted to annihilate the human race, but then he realized there wouldn't be anybody left to worship him. So he decided to cut the spherical creatures in half, leaving two arms, two legs, and one sexual organ on each half. Then he told Apollo, the most beautiful of the gods, to reconstruct their faces and sew up their stomachs, so they would look a little more presentable when they went back to Earth, and so their scars would remind them not to be so proud. From then on, there were no more powerful, arrogant spheres rolling around. The new, chopped-in-half beings found that their population had doubled, but they felt terribly weak and distraught about the loss of their other halves. The myth ends with the poor beings condemned to wander around for eternity, desperately searching for their soul mates.

As you struggle through your quest for love, you're not too different from a half sphere trying to become whole. According to Plato, the human desire for love dates back to this ancient era. In this myth, love is much more than a bubbly, love-at-first-sight feeling. Love is what makes you complete. In writing about the myth, Plato wanted to help people understand that "eros," a Greek word for love, is a force that has been a part of humanity since ancient times, a longing first felt by beings who wanted to numb the pain of being split in half. Each person is the other half of another. Because this desire for completion is built into you, no number of disastrous dates can stop you from hoping it will all work out eventually. As long as you are without your other half, the search will go on—at your friends' weddings, on dating apps, and everywhere else. You will keep on trying to find that lost half, even if it means putting yourself through a lot of confusion and misadventures. No matter how discouraged you get, you will always have an overwhelming desire to find that one person who makes you feel complete and at peace with yourself.

Plato's myth of Aristophanes tells us we all have a soul mate waiting for us somewhere in the world. Someone unique, irreplaceable, perfectly matched to the essence of who we are. But in order to find our other half, we have to search—and we search by trying out different paths, by meeting and falling in love with different people, by putting ourselves out there to find where our other half might be hiding.

The next time your second cousin's friend's roommate wants to introduce you to somebody, don't beat yourself up for diving headfirst into romantic daydreams. Don't listen to your naysaying friends. Instead, practice your witty remarks, pick out an outfit you love, and remember that this undying hope for love is just a desire to find a missing other half. You're not crazy; you're just a Platonist.

Plato at a Glance (427–348 BCE)

Plato was born in Athens in 427 BCE. An aristocrat with a lofty education, he became a disciple of Socrates. Because Socrates refused to record his own philosophies, Plato documented their discussions, always featuring his master's style of teaching in an effort to directly engage the reader with philosophical questions. Plato's works are dynamic, and reading them feels almost interactive. He covers everything from politics to love. He also alludes to many myths and points out the difference between the perceptible world and the world of ideas. He spent time in Sicily, during the reign of Dionysius I of Syracuse, but when he got in trouble with the court, he left on a boat and was caught in a terrible storm. After washing up on the island of Aegina, he was sold into slavery but then was freed by a friend. He founded a school called the Academy, where Aristotle was a student. Thousands of years later, Plato is still considered one of the most essential thinkers in Western philosophy.

The Book You Need in a Crisis: <u>Symposium</u>

While enjoying a huge banquet (and many goblets of wine), Socrates and his guests take turns articulating what feeds our souls: love! Plato chronicled the whole conversation in his book *Symposium.*

Philosophy to the Rescue

- Love is what you feel when you find your other half—the person who makes you complete and at peace.
- Desire fuels the search for a soul mate.
- Having faith in love is not childish or silly. Keep searching for the person you truly belong with.

All Things Must Pas(cal)

Or, Bringing Time into Focus

*y*ou're the kind of person who never arrives on time. You're either too early or too late—it's like a superpower. You don't let time control you; you control it. You don't understand why people get so overwrought about the passage of time and the onset of old age. You're not worried about getting old, because you know you'll have complete control over that too. Your hair will turn gray when *you* decide the time is right. You don't have to follow any schedule but your own. You will keep wearing the sneakers you've had since you were fifteen until the end of time. Each passing year will only make you cooler than you were the year before. You will be young at heart and hip forever.

So it didn't bother you when, on a recent business trip, you were checking into a hotel and you accidently signed your name on the line that said "Today's Date." It was just a tiny mistake. Your brain was busy doing a million other things. The next week you went to see a marvelous Lithuanian film, except that you didn't understand any of it because you couldn't read the subtitles. It wasn't your fault. They were written in some unintelligible font.

A few days later you saw a stranger waving to you from across the street. At first you thought they were crazy, but then you realized the person was actually a friend of yours. You have started to wonder if maybe you should see a doctor. You aren't worried, just genuinely confused as to why you're having these problems. It must be that the stress at work is getting to you. You set a reminder to block out a relaxing weekend in your schedule—soon, but not right now, because you're too busy.

Then one morning the truth slaps you in the face. You're sitting at your desk and you can't read your emails. Your vision has always been as good as a pilot's, but now you're nose-diving. No more excuses. It's time to face facts: you need glasses. You're taken aback. How can this be happening? How dare your eyes have the audacity to weaken? You remember how your parents always used to forget their glasses on the coffee table or in the glove compartment, and how they'd wearily ask you to read the menu to them at restaurants. You remember the too-strict, bespectacled elementary school teacher whose glasses you used to hide for fun (she deserved it). There's no way you're as old as your parents or that teacher. You're practically still a teenager!

Of course the truth is too unbearable, so you quickly decide to go with contact lenses: socially acceptable and physically tolerable, or so you think. You practice poking your finger into your eye, but you can't. Doing that every morning will be horrifically traumatic. You will have to get actual glasses. You start to panic—not because you're worried about how the frames will look but because you can't believe that from now on your eyes will need an artificial appendage in order to function correctly.

Eventually you resolve to go to the optometrist with the feeling that you're signing your own death warrant. You have been robbed of your power. You no longer have control over the passage of time. You've always surfed through the stages of your life, never letting anyone else's rhythm interrupt your own. But it turns out that time—which you trusted like a lover—has been cheating on you all along.

All of a sudden you don't feel comfortable in your sneakers anymore, even though they're the same style you have always worn. The accessory perched upon your nose is forcing you to look back at all the years of your life that have passed you by. You have always been impatient, but now all you want to do is make time slow down, but you can't. Suddenly you feel old and feeble. You scrutinize the lines on your face, like a geologist, examining each little crack and crevice on the surface of your skin. You don't know what to do. You don't want to leave your house. The past makes you nostalgic; the future seems grim. What is happening to you? Is time finally taking its revenge for all those years you ignored it? You desperately need someone to wind back your internal clock.

What Would Pascal Have to Say About All of This?

When he was nineteen, Blaise Pascal built a basic calculator just by fiddling with some gears. If he could do that, he can definitely help you find some clarity about the number of years you've been alive. He wrote a lot about the relationship between humans and time in his book *Pensées,* or *Thoughts.*

His main point is that humans do not live in the moment. So much of our time is spent remembering the past or making plans for the future—all while we casually dismiss the present. It's as if living in the here and now is only for people with nothing better to do. We're always late for something or early for something else, and never simply on time. We never really appreciate that time is passing—until a wrinkle or an optometrist points it out to us. In order to break this habit, we need to figure out why it's ingrained in us. Why are we so eager to escape the present? Pascal analyzes people's internal mechanisms piece by piece, looking for the grain of sand that could be stuck in the gears.

First, Pascal looks at desire. We so desperately want to experience incredible things and we get so excited about our plans that when they actually come to pass, they often seem disappointing after all the time and energy we spent anticipating them. It's like when we spend months waiting for a surprise and then we're underwhelmed when it finally arrives because we've been thinking about it for so long. The present moment speeds past, leaving us with this feeling of frustration. So we gear ourselves toward the future again, which we decide will be so much more fulfilling than the present. We hit FAST-FORWARD to try to put some distance between ourselves and our disappointments. After all, we don't want to dwell on the mundane letdowns of the present. We want to keep facing forward and to feel in control of our own destinies.

We often reject the present because it doesn't live up to expectations. But Pascal's theory also applies when the opposite happens: when the present moment is too beautiful, the surprise too perfect. Dreams that come true can be just as hard to deal with as dreams that are never realized. Pascal points out how temperamental humans can be. When everything is going well, we want to freeze time and bask in that happiness forever; but seeing as that's impossible, we become obsessed instead with the fact that at every second the timer on our happiness is ticking away. We can't enjoy our happiness because we feel like an all-powerful hourglass is running out.

Basically, you're always going to be frustrated by time. The present moment—whether it's disappointing or amazing—stresses you out. When you live with this kind of attitude, you have no anchor in reality. You don't know who you are, what your life is, or even how old you are. If you don't have a point of reference or an understanding of the way your life is progressing, a pair of glasses becomes a terrifying wake-up call. You're suddenly thrown into the present, which you've been trying to escape. So what should you do? Crowd your schedule with distractions? Start planning your own funeral? Thankfully, Pascal has a better idea.

The nice thing about time is that it passes, but it is always with you. So it's never too late to change your attitude toward time, and that is exactly what Pascal can help you do. All things must pass, everyone is going to die anyway, and there's nothing you can do about that, so you should put your energy toward changing your actions, which you have complete agency over. You can't stop time, but you can control the way you move through it. If the present moment is disappointing, try to make it more exciting. Conversely, if the present moment is overwhelmingly happy, stop for a second to observe it and let the joy sink in.

Getting older is just a matter of learning to adjust. At the end of the day, you should realize that it's the present moment that needs laser surgery, not you. Don't despair. Instead, pick out a stylish pair of frames, put your glasses on, and watch your life come into focus. You'll finally be able to see the beautiful contours of reality in high definition.

Pascal at a Glance (1623–1662)

Born in 1623 in Clermont-Ferrand, France, Blaise Pascal was definitely a child prodigy. With encouragement from his father, he learned about everything he could. Science and math were his main passions before he began studying theology. At only nineteen years old he invented a calculator and was a pioneer in the field of probability. By the age of thirty, however, all those numbers went to his head and he had a spiritual meltdown, suffering from hallucinations. After this experience, he became focused on religion. He developed a philosophy based on the premise that humans are inherently gloomy and they can only find interior peace and true happiness if they can connect with God. Pascal's health was fragile. He dealt with chronic pain, which slowed down his writing. His two major works, published shortly after his death, were as precocious and intelligent as he was.

The Book You Need in a Crisis: <u>Pensées (Thoughts)</u>

Everyone loves a good existential crisis, and Pascal was an expert on the subject. In this book, published in 1669, he points out that when you're unsure of your greater purpose, it's easy for your day-to-day existence to become sad and meaningless. You search for a distraction from the present, always reminiscing or waiting for the next thing to come along. *Pensées* can help you break this cycle and find peace and happiness within.

Philosophy to the Rescue

- You have trouble living in the moment. This is either because you're afraid of being disappointed or because you're stressed about time moving too fast. When you worry about the past or the future, the present passes you by before you even realize it.
- There is no need to be afraid of the present. After all, it's where you're living your life.
- Getting old is a good thing, because with age you learn to live in and appreciate the present.

Levinas Before Xanax

Or, Learning to Love the Other

$\mathcal{F}$or all these years you've kept it safe in a corner of your desk drawer. It's a little talisman you sometimes come across when you're hunting for a Post-it note. Every time you find it, you stop for a moment, misty-eyed, and hold the tiny hospital bracelet that was clipped off so long ago. This little piece of plastic is like the ticket stub to a movie of your past life. The bracelet doesn't just make you nostalgic; it sends you to another era—a time when the soundtrack to your life was merry-go-round music and the biggest tragedies you had to deal with were lost toys or fallen chocolate ice cream cones.

You love children. Even before you had your own, you were always the first to join the kids' table to play Monopoly and the last one to tell them to get out of the swimming pool. You've combed through dozens of books on pedagogy, and you have strong opinions about the impact of video games and social media on children's lives.

You've always been a model parent, both responsible and kind. You let them skateboard, but you were strict about good manners. You always clapped for the little shows they put on from behind the sofa before going to sleep. Sometimes the shows were weirder than Celine Dion on LSD, but your support never wavered. You never looked at your watch or yawned while you read them stories. You were a birthday party savant, an expert in after-school activities, and a playhouse connoisseur. Basically, childhood was your kingdom, and your little blond subject was as sweet and gentle as could be.

The seasons changed as quickly as social dynamics on the playground. Through it all, people looked to you as an example of stress-free parenting. You never saw children as unpredictable little monsters the way other parents did. You saw them as adorable, easygoing angels. Even if you weren't picking your child up from school quite as often, you still felt that the bond was as strong as ever. Sure, there had been one or two comments about your outfits, but you understood this was all part of the process—just a bit of intergenerational conflict, as benign as something from a sitcom.

And so you're confused when you open the door to your

apartment one night after a grueling business trip—you're exhausted from traveling, so you think maybe you're hearing things, but, no, someone is banging around in your kitchen. Are you being robbed? Are you in the wrong apartment? Your eyes scan the room as you try to put together a coherent narrative and figure out what's happening. There's a sock on the marble countertop, next to a knocked-over bottle of ketchup, next to a plugged-in hairdryer, next to a bag of sour-cream-and-onion chips, next to a jumble of Polaroid photos. The sink is piled high with dirty dishes. The couch in the living room has become a clothes rack. You're trying to puzzle through all of this when suddenly a person nearly as tall as you appears in the doorway. This person says to you in a less-than-friendly tone, "Why are you home so early? And why did you take my phone charger? Seriously, are you trying to ruin my life?" Who is this stranger? Where is your little treasure, who once wore knit hats with panda ears? How did everything change so quickly? You can't deny it any longer: you're the parent of a teenager.

Being the caring parent you are, you have read all sorts of articles about teenagers—about their oppositional tendencies and their need for independence. You do understand that the point of childhood is for children to grow. You've even learned to communicate through texts and emojis. But right now you are at a loss. What you're feeling cannot be conveyed with a smiley face emoji. This person in your apartment is not a child or even an adolescent dealing with a hormone overload. This person is a stranger—a complete stranger whose dialect consists only of "You suck!" peppered with "Duh!" and the occasional muffled "Ughh" shouted into the pillows on the couch. You understand none of it.

Ever since you realized what is happening, you've been in a state of shock. You've been laid off from your job as the best parent ever. Like an anthropologist, you observe this creature moving through your apartment. You have absolutely no idea how to connect with them. Monopoly games can't help you anymore. You've tried to learn everything you can about today's youth—their ideologies and their fashion choices—but you can't keep up. As soon as you realize that their wearing a sweatshirt three sizes too big is a conscious decision and not a mistake, they're on to something else. They cut holes in their new skinny jeans, which you ironed with loving care. They wear T-shirts that say "WTF?" and "Don't Talk to Me."

You don't want to overreact, but your little angel really has gone over to the dark side—they've become an impossible-to-solve riddle. When they inform you that you are the worst, most embarrassing parent in the entire galaxy, you try to decide between strangling them with their little hospital bracelet and getting your own shirt that says "WTF?"

because you want to know WTF happened to your sweet little panda child.

What Would Levinas Have to Say About All of This?

Teenage Emmanuel Levinas probably wasn't the rebellious type, but as an adult, he came up with some ideas about morality that are very relevant to your situation. He grappled with questions of how to deal with people as they change—and if changing were a sport, teenagers would be the champions every season.

Throughout his works, Levinas talked about a concept he calls the Other. This simple term is profoundly important to his philosophy. The Other is the person in front of you who has the nerve to not be anything like you. You can't know what they're thinking. The fact that you can't understand them frustrates you. You love to hate them. They contradict you. Basically, the Other is anyone different from you, simply because they're not you. This Other can be anyone: your parents, your partner, your boss, someone on the subway, your neighbor across the street, or, right now, the teenager living in your apartment.

Levinas talks about the paradoxes in relationships with a clarity that characterizes all of his philosophy. He describes how infuriating the Other is. The Other never reacts the way you expect them to. They have completely different tastes. They are strange, and they are a stranger. And yet for some odd reason you always seek out their presence—they fascinate you. Instead of avoiding this frustrating Other, which would be a logical response, you try to get as close to them as you possibly can. You would do anything to understand what makes them tick. You hover around them, trying to gather information about them with more determination and focus every day.

This contradiction between frustration and a desperate need for connection takes on its truest form in a parent–teenager relationship. You could just leave your teenager alone while they whine about how annoying you are, holding a phone in one hand and a video game controller in the other. You could just stand back and wait for the storm of hormones to pass. But instead, you spend tons of time and energy running after them, terrified by the fact that your own flesh and blood is so different from you. You can try to understand their language and the music they listen to, or you can do the opposite and try to force your love of reading on them, but neither approach will make a difference. No amount of conversations, books about how to raise teenagers, or bonding activities will make this relationship easy. The Other will remain an incomprehensible enigma and will continue to roll their eyes at you for a few years, but believe it or not, that is actually a good thing.

This is where Levinas comes in. The rough patch between you and your teenager is actually something to celebrate; it's what gives your relationship a future. The Other is nothing like you—that's why you're so passionately interested in them. Trying to understand the Other gives meaning to your life. It's your intense physical and emotional reaction to the Other that makes them such an essential part of your existence. You don't understand the Other, but you learn to understand yourself by observing them. Your "I," your sense of self, is defined by the gestures, expressions, and words of this stranger who intrigues you, torments you, and mystifies you. By observing your teenager in a state of chaos, you begin to better understand yourself. If you were all alone, your life would be a lot more peaceful and your apartment would be a lot less messy, but you wouldn't have the same opportunities to evolve, reflect, and become a better version of yourself.

At the end of the day, you love the Other so much that you're willing to set aside your exasperation in order to take care of them. Maybe the fact that they're different from you—the very reason they annoy you—is also the reason you feel so much sympathy and responsibility for them.

Of course you get sick of trying to decipher their half-asleep monosyllabic grumbling, but you will always wait up to make sure they get home safely from that party at their friend's house—the friend whose address they refused to give you. You will always make sure the comforter on their bed smells as sweet as it did when they were a baby.

To interact with a teenager is to interact with the Other, and you don't need to understand the Other to feel a deep love and responsibility for them. This is important to bear in mind when interacting with anyone of any age. Every important relationship goes through rough patches. People can be ungrateful or can change suddenly, but no matter what's going on, Levinas's advice is the same: let the Other know you are there for them, even in moments of conflict, even when you feel like there's no point. This is a valuable approach to take to all types of relationships—it's an implicit pact you make with the Other as soon as they enter your life. By the power of empathy and love, someday the Other will agree to play Monopoly with you again, just like old times.

Levinas at a Glance (1906–1995)

Born in Lithuania in 1906, Emmanuel Levinas received an education influenced by Judaism. He always preferred reasoning and questions to answers. While in exile in Ukraine, he developed a passion for Russian literature; Dostoyevsky was especially important to his philosophy. In 1923, he presented his philosophical studies in Strasbourg, toggling between several languages in order to get at the particularities of his ideas. He met Martin Heidegger during a trip to Germany and then lived in Paris for several years, becoming a French citizen in 1939. He was drafted and later became a prisoner of war in a German camp for five years. Witnessing such extreme human suffering had a profound impact on Levinas. His belief in the importance of connecting with the Other, and his belief that morality comes from caring, grew even stronger. His philosophy is an ethical code based in altruism that says every person must feel responsible for the Other. This was a new idea in contemporary philosophy, making Levinas an extremely important philosopher long after his death in 1995.

The Book You Need in a Crisis: *Totality and Infinity*

In 1963, Levinas published his thesis, *Totality and Infinity*, long after his own angsty adolescent days. He explains in it that we can find the depth we seek only through our interactions with others. With the intensity and conviction of a friend telling it like it is, Levinas points out the absurdity of hatred. When we hate someone, we're torn between cutting them out of our lives and trying, with everything we have, to understand them. This mix of rejection and attachment is what makes hatred absurd. You can't have your cake and hate it too. Levinas insists that putting your hatred aside and embracing the Other is the best way forward.

Philosophy to the Rescue

- Others will always seem strange to you, teenagers especially, simply because they are wired differently.

- You can learn about yourself from the Other precisely because they are different from you.
- Morality means caring for the Other with empathy and taking responsibility for them without expecting anything in return.

A Bone to Pick with Heidegger

*Or, What Happens
When Your Dog Dies*

*Y*ou just happened to be in the right place at the right time. Your friend made you go with her to the animal shelter. It was like those cheesy stories where someone comes along to support their friend at an audition and then ends up getting cast in the lead role. That's how it happened—he picked you out of the crowd and you were a goner. His big, dark eyes, gazing at you from behind the bars of a dirty kennel—they just about killed you. With his paws pushing against the cage, he seemed to be waiting for you and only you, loyal from the start. You never thought you would get a dog. That life simply wasn't for you. You knew getting a pet wasn't something to do on a whim—it's a huge, and stressful, commitment. But that morning, despite all of your hesitations, you had no choice. You had to hold him in your arms, even if it meant he would chew up your life. You drove home, not fully understanding how important the little bundle of joy in the back seat would become for you. Your family was shocked. You told them you were probably just taking care of him for a few weeks, knowing full well that "a few weeks" would turn into a lifetime.

You had to come up with a perfect name for such a perfect dog. To narrow it down, you decided his name should start with a *g*. Your friends came up with all sorts of ridiculous names, which you considered insults to the canine race. You didn't listen to any of them. You decided to name your dog Gustave Johnson. You thought it was important for him to have a last name, for the sake of his dignity.

In no time, Gustave Johnson made his mark on every corner of his kingdom, also known as your apartment. Lick by slobbery lick, the two of you built a life together. It was a beautiful partnership. Gustave Johnson filled your days with wonder and with weird smells. Each morning you woke up to the rhythm of his breathing at the foot of the bed. You were always amazed by how flexible he was. He would roll around frenetically on your bed, tucking his head under his tail, while you struggled just to get out of bed. He had the spirit of a star athlete. He ran after you on bike rides and went swimming with you in the summers. He was the perfect confidant. He would listen to you talk about your deepest, saddest secrets, and he really seemed to understand you, flopping his ears around with compassion.

Your relationship with Gustave Johnson wasn't perfect. You hated taking him out at dawn and late at night, especially in terrible weather. When it rained, the smell of the soggy fur on his butt mixed with the stench of old dog food made you want to wipe down your whole apartment with bleach.

Because you had to go home and let him out into the yard, he helped you escape all kinds of annoying conversations, interminable lunches, and work events. He was the all-powerful excuse for anything. He was a magnet for smiles from strangers and likes on Instagram—eventually you set up a Gustave Johnson Instagram account so the whole world could enjoy his goofiness.

Traveling with Gustave Johnson helped you hone your negotiation skills. Every summer you got to practice the speech you delivered at hotel front desks, about how your dog was a perfect angel. When someone found muddy paw prints on the white hallway carpet, you reacted like the parent of a young child: apologetic and taken aback. You went to ridiculous lengths for him. Once, he left his favorite toy at a highway rest stop and you drove for miles to get it back. It's true that sometimes you wanted to yell at him, like when he knocked over dishes and houseplants. You even threatened to leave him behind at the park once or twice, but in your heart, you knew you couldn't live without him.

And then one fall morning, as you waited for him to begin his morning routine of tearing up your curtains, you realized he was late. You found him huddled in his little basket. His once-perky ears looked lifeless. His once-sparkling eyes were weary. The veterinarian, who was usually so dismissive of your questions about dog food brands, gave you a verdict right away. Gustave Johnson was terminally ill. You refused to believe it. He was supposed to be by your side for life. Surely your sidekick could beat this, or maybe the veterinarian had made a mistake. You talked to specialists. You remained in denial and tried every crazy treatment you could think of, but your hope was not enough to cure Gustave Johnson.

And finally, despite your unwavering faith in him, all those nights you spent scrolling through pet-owner forums online, the schemes you came up with to sneak his medicine into dabs of peanut butter, despite everything, he left you. No more wet nose, no more whining, no more puppy eyes to make you drop whatever you were doing. There is now an unbearable emptiness in your apartment. Your dog, your truest friend and ally, is gone. You have been left alone in a dizzying and barkless void.

What Would Heidegger Have to Say About All of This?

Martin Heidegger—one of the more anxious, worried, and existentially minded philosophers—wasn't much of a dog person, but his ideas can still help you come to terms with the loss of your furry best friend. Heidegger wrote about how people spend most of their lives bogged down by boring details and meaningless chatter. Building on that premise, Heidegger is going to help you rediscover authenticity in your life, and make it through this sad time.

Since death plays an important role in Heidegger's philosophy, coping with the death of your dog will help you understand his ideas more deeply. Heidegger can show you how to turn your grief into an opportunity for self-exploration and a way to think about where your life is going. In order for this to work, you need to look at death head-on.

Heidegger noticed that most people view death as an ordinary occurrence that's barely even worth discussing since it happens to all of us in the end. Why not focus on the frivolous and futile business of everyday life when the alternative is just waiting around for death? We know we can't prevent death, so we ignore it. If death is nothing but a distant concern—a vague time limit on life, represented by a skull on a teenager's hoodie—we can avoid worrying about it. We can cheerfully go about our lives, taking care of our familial, professional, and social responsibilities, without the specter of death hanging over us.

But there it is: when you stare at your dog's empty bed, death is no longer just an abstract concept. Death is a concrete absence of cuddles and soft fur. Death has arrived at your doorstep, and it's impossible to treat it with the same indifference you used to. You mourn the death of your dog, but even more than that, you mourn something Heidegger called Dasein, or existence—a strange word for a simple thing: being, and everything that makes an individual unique. A death isn't just a tragedy. It can be a wake-up call, a reason to start living a more authentic and present life, one that isn't drowned out by thousands of to-do lists and anxieties about things that don't matter. When your dog dies, you stop worrying about stains on the carpet and ripped-up curtains, and start thinking more deeply about how your dog affected you.

For Heidegger, your Dasein can be broken into a few parts. These parts of yourself make you a "being toward death," which is just a fancy way of saying a person destined to die, as all people are. Even though this might seem depressing, Heidegger didn't think of it that way. He just wanted to show us that death is a part of human reality. By trying to escape the inevitable or pretending it doesn't bother us, we're actually running away from our own nature. Refusing to think about death is refusing a fundamental human anxiety—the anxiety that our life will end one day. Accepting and learning to think about this anxiety after the death of your dog isn't just a way to understand yourself; it's a way to regain authenticity in your life, a way to admit to yourself that the end is unavoidable, and a way to think about death as a part of life. As soon as a being—human or dog—is born, they are old enough to die.

To live an authentic life, according to Heidegger, you need to recognize and accept that death is coming—and you need to accept it honestly, without fear. Being aware of loss and meeting it with bravery and clarity will allow you to live a more meaningful life. So even if the loss of your furry friend makes you want to curl up next to his bed and hold on to his chew toys until the pain goes away, you have to resist the impulse to stay in denial. Gustave Johnson's death is an opportunity to be brave in a dog-eat-dog world and to face the reality of loss in all its cruelty. Also, wouldn't Dasein be a great name for a new dog?

Heidegger at a Glance (1889–1976)

Martin Heidegger was born in 1889 in a little German village called Messkirch. He grew up in a very Catholic family, and as a teenager, he devoured religious and philosophical texts in equal measure. Later, determined to become a priest, he abandoned philosophy, believing it was incompatible with religion. Eventually he changed his mind, and in 1916, he became a personal assistant to the philosopher Edmund Husserl, who shared Heidegger's love of phenomenology—the study of human consciousness. Heidegger admired Husserl but didn't work for him for long. In 1923, Heidegger became a professor at the University of Marburg, where he had a profound impact on his students. Many of them went on to become important thinkers in their own right, like Hannah Arendt, Leo Strauss, and Hans Jonas. Most of Heidegger's work centered around questions of what it means to be and to exist. The 1930s were a sobering era politically but a very rich one philosophically. The turmoil of those years would be dealt with for generations to come but coincided with the emergence of important ideas about metaphysics.

The Book You Need in a Crisis: *Being and Time*

Martin Heidegger found new ways to be meta. *Being and Time,* while not exactly a breezy beach read, forms part of the foundation of contemporary metaphysics. In it, Heidegger explores the meaning of life by looking critically at how the passage of time allows you to be in touch with your own existence. Anything but morbid, the ability to face death head-on actually helps you understand life in new ways.

Philosophy to the Rescue

- You lose your way in life when you focus on fleeting, pointless things.
- Every individual embodies Dasein and is a unique being.
- Being aware of death isn't depressing. In fact, it allows you to find meaning in your life and to take advantage of the time you have, instead of spending it on things that don't matter.

When You Kant Get Over a Breakup

Or, Separating Reason and Passion

*I*t's 4:24 p.m. You're jumping up and down with excitement. You feel like you're back in high school sitting through one of those boring classes that seemed to last for centuries. It's as if time has stepped in chewing gum and has stopped moving forward. You literally can't wait. You haven't seen him for ten days. You each went on separate vacations. It was the longest time you've been deprived of each other's company since you started dating. During your vacation, you couldn't stop thinking about him. You bought an absurd number of silly souvenirs for him to ease the pain of being apart, and now, finally, you're going to be reunited. You feel jittery. You pace around your apartment and call friends to distract yourself. You arrange and re-arrange the dishes in your cabinets to try to pass the time. You feel like a child overwhelmed at an amusement park.

You can't concentrate. You can't think about anything but the moment when you'll see him.

At 5:00 p.m. you decide you will explode if you wait any longer, so you start walking to the coffee shop where you've planned to meet him. As you stride down the sidewalk, you replay your favorite romantic moments with him over the past month—the late nights, running out of your offices to steal a moment together, laughing for no reason, deep discussions over dinner. The two of you make even the most romantic of romantic comedies seem dull. Your relationship is the perfect love story. You're living the cliché that people think is unrealistic, if they have never been in love like this. Your friends complain that you never go out with them anymore and you have your head in the clouds. They say this relationship is getting in the way of other parts of your life, but they don't understand.

Your parents worry that it's moving too fast. Other friends say that he's a bad person, that they don't like the way he treats you. Your sister keeps telling you he's not the one. You're convinced they're all just jealous and bitter. They're used to you always being the single one, and they can't understand your incredible bond. You don't listen to any of them. You're blinded by his gorgeous face, his wit and charm. It doesn't matter what people say; you would follow him anywhere. You want to do everything he wants to do. You don't care that his lifestyle pushes you out of your comfort zone and makes you do things that used to be against your morals. You feel more powerful with him by your side than you have ever felt before. You admit that he's like a hurricane, but you love being caught in the storm, and you want to be a part of this meteorological chaos forever, for better or for worse.

You arrive at the coffee shop. You're way too early, of course, but you don't mind. You're just happy to be there. The décor is cozy. It's perfect for a romantic date. You can't stop imagining those first glorious seconds when you will be reunited. It will be a moment to remember forever—a moment when relief, desire, and excitement all mix together. Thinking about it makes your heart beat faster than any cardio workout. You meticulously planned your outfit for this date. You don't want to look too dolled up, you want to look nonchalant and cool, but you also want to floor him when he walks in and sees his gorgeous partner. Even the barista notices how happy you are. Nothing can shake your confidence in the future. And then eventually, off in the distance, you see him. He pushes past the other people in the café to get to you. You're overjoyed and ready to throw yourself into his arms, Julia Roberts style.

But as he gets closer to the table, you realize he is in no mood to be Richard Gere. He must be tired, which is understandable, but still, you wish he would hug you. It's the first pang—a little, disappointed electroshock. But it's nothing compared to what happens next. He doesn't pick you up or twirl you around. He just looks at you coldly. He mutters something about how he needs to take some time for himself right now. "It's not you. It's me." The language of breaking up is as banal as the language of love at first sight.

What was supposed to be a romantic comedy has turned into a tragedy. The people around you are the audience—some look embarrassed; others eye you with sympathy. Your boyfriend, now ex-boyfriend, decides to leave you at the table. He stands up and walks away without even paying for your coffee. You're completely crushed. You hold out hope that he'll come back, which just makes it worse. Finally, you realize he's never coming back. Your heart beats slowly. It's sad and confused.

By 6:30 p.m. you're devastated. Your heart is heavy and your eyes are wet. You feel like the last few months of your life have been some elaborate, nasty trick. How could he have changed his mind so quickly? How could he have seemed so sincere? You can't call your friends because they'll just tell you they were right all along. You don't know what to do or what to think. You don't know anything except that you're going to need a shot of vodka and some solid philosophy to help you calm down.

What Would Kant Have to Say About All of This?

Immanuel Kant probably wasn't too familiar with the trials and tribulations of love. His life was pretty drama-free. Most of his days were identical—all he did was meditate and teach. Nothing, not crushes or breakups or other matters of love, got in the way of his intellectual life. His existence was centered on reason and how to best make use of it. However, you can draw inspiration from this way of thinking to heal your broken heart and protect it from the next romantic crisis.

Kant praised reason and condemned passion. He also described how each of them works. He defined reason as everything that comes from reflection and not from lived experience. This means that we don't need to be confronted by something—we don't need to live it, touch it, and feel it—to be able to think about it. Reason is a beacon of light, a tool that gives us the power to analyze, to zoom out, to reflect—to better understand situations and react to them in calm, reasonable ways. Passion, on the other hand, is a feeling that no amount of rational thought or action can control. Reason has no power over passion. According to Kant, passion is not simply an emotion but a disease of the soul. This passion, this spiritual gangrene that flares up when we start falling in love, makes us crazy—we hope and wait and idealize everything. Our reason crumbles when this fever spikes. We lose any ability to think clearly. We're removed from reality.

In his book *Anthropology from a Pragmatic Point of View,* Kant takes these ideas a step further. In addition to explaining his definition of passion, he explains all of the risks we take when we yield to passion. He says that passionate love is dangerous because it inevitably leads to us acting in immoral ways. But what is the connection between passion and immorality? It's pretty simple: passion prevents all reflection. When we are in love, we lose the ability to hear the reasonable voice in our head or the advice of our parents and friends. We lose our ability to compare, measure, choose, confront, or question anything. We are caught in a storm. We frantically count the minutes until the next time we will see our beloved. When we're not with the person we love, we feel fragile. This conflagration eats away at every part of our lives. We are deprived of the tools we need to exercise our morals, because, according to Kant, moral law's only base is reason. To be moral is to act in such a way that our actions could be emulated universally. Basically, this means that before we do something, we should ask ourselves if the act we are about to perform will be good for everyone involved. To do this, we need to be able to put our reason to work. We can't just listen to our heart beating like crazy when someone kisses us and says they love us. We have to be reasonable. Reason and morality go hand in hand. If we lose track of one, we can't expect to keep the other.

But that's not all. When we are completely overtaken by passion, unable to reason and to take a step back from situations, we forget what is good for us. We find ourselves attached to another person without really having the opportunity to rationally think about whether or not our actions make sense. Passion makes us slaves to something that is outside ourselves. Kant explains that when we are consumed by passion for another person, we are letting ourselves be cheated by a feeling that is not based on anything stable. Once the honeymoon phase is over and the relationship starts to feel normal, the passion falls away and we're at risk of crying alone in a coffee shop after being dumped. Passion gives us a kind of vertigo. It makes us lose ourselves in another person. The idea of doing anything to separate ourselves from our reason is inconceivable for Kant.

However, even though he encourages us to break up with passion, Kant is not saying that we should be eternally single. Actually, he draws an interesting distinction between passion and love, which is very comforting. He says that passion is false, unhealthy, and ephemeral. But love is real. Love is a product of a relationship that's reasonable and lasting. Love is not something negative or something to be afraid of. A person who loves another person can stay clear-sighted and can support their feelings of love with free will instead of just imagined, perfect ideas. Real love is less turbulent and more solid than passion. Not recognizing that there is a difference between love and passion, and renouncing both to avoid suffering, is depriving yourself of the opportunity to create harmony between your reason and your heart.

It's time to stop being controlled by passion. You need to dry your tears, gather your strength, and stop expecting your life to follow the plotline of a romantic comedy. No more giddiness, no more passion. It's time to strive for love. And the journey will be more beautiful, longer lasting, and stronger than any fleeting infatuation.

Kant at a Glance (1724–1804)

Born in Königsberg in 1724, Immanuel Kant was the fourth of eleven children. He had a modest, very religious upbringing, and he never left the region where he was born. In college, he became interested in Isaac Newton's scientific theories. The idea that one could do science a priori, meaning without actually experiencing it, was fascinating for young Kant. He was a major figure in the German Enlightenment and one of the first people to teach philosophy at a university. He is known for scheduling each of his days identically. He had no family or romantic life. He taught courses and dedicated the rest of his time to his philosophical work—asking himself questions about morality, aesthetics, and politics. He spent eleven years writing his most famous work, *Critique of Pure Reason,* published in 1781. The work shows why metaphysics cannot lead to a real understanding of the world. In 1804, Kant died in his hometown. His last words were "It is good." His contributions to philosophy are still very important today.

The Book You Need in a Crisis:
Anthropology from a Pragmatic Point of View

While you can't unload your breakup angst on Professor Kant, this book will help you see reason. Published in 1798, *Anthropology from a Pragmatic Point of View* is a collection of lectures he gave during his anthropology course. In it, he teaches the concept of focusing on greater questions, such as the practical applications of philosophy and humanity's place in the world. It's a great introduction to Kant's ideas and touches on almost every aspect of human existence—love included.

Philosophy to the Rescue

- Passion makes you lose your ability to reason and makes you so agitated that you aren't able to think clearly about your decisions.
- Passion deprives you of your morality and your freedom. When passion consumes you, your reason has no power

to stop it. You think only about another person and forget to think about yourself.

- There is a difference between love and passion. Passion leads to suffering, but love is stable and durable. Love, like all other positive aspects of existence, is founded in reason.

Bergson Launches a Start-Up

Or, Working to Create Yourself

You finally do it. On a Friday in September, everyone else is looking forward to the weekend, when they'll have a fleeting and false sense of freedom, but not you. You hand in your ID with a dramatic flourish, hoping the security cameras catch this historic moment. You've been carrying that employee badge around for more than twelve years, but it's all over now. You throw the little plastic rectangle on the front desk, with barely a thought for the photocopy credit you never used up. You feel so free and so proud of yourself for quitting this job before it got the better of your mental health and your soul. Those 8:15 a.m. meetings? Done. Those brain-rotting Power-Point presentations? Wiped from your schedule. Hiding your phone under your desk to check Facebook? Never again. You are finished dealing with boring chitchat at the coffee machine and eating sad salads at your desk. The time has come to live your best life and be your own boss. You're going to make new business cards of your very own as physical proof of your professional and spiritual growth.

Freedom tastes so sweet. As you gathered up the last of your things and left your soulless office for the last time, you looked at your coworkers with compassion and sympathy. How sad, how passé, to work for someone else. You can't wait to wear your casual Friday clothes from Monday on. You can almost taste the communal cold-brew coffee and organic granola you'll eat in co-working spaces. You will work whenever and wherever you want to. The weekend can come on a Tuesday if you decide you need a break. The start-up life is the life for you. As long as you have 5G Wi-Fi, you'll be unstoppable. You'll finally get to incorporate your passions into your professional life. You're so excited to spend your nights effervescing with ideas. You're going to turn your living room into a creative sanctuary, and you'll throw out that horrible messenger bag you used to haul around. It's the start of a new era. You'll be working from home now. Everything you do will fill you with energy. You'll be able to control every aspect of your life—your future, your schedule, everything. Your parents congratulate you (even though the whole thing worries them), your friends are jealous, and your romantic conquests admire your entrepreneurial spirit.

For the first few days, you're full of joy and confidence. You feel like you have wings on the back of your tech-bro sweatshirt. Your new favorite hobby is fiddling with your website's color scheme. You never realized just how creative you were until you started making your own organizational flow charts. No matter who you talk to, you find a way to let them know that the life of an entrepreneur is glorious.

But...after an idyllic six months, you start to develop some habits that make it hard to just sit on your couch brainstorming and feeling cool. You become obsessed with your inbox, checking and refreshing it constantly, like your life depends on it (and maybe it does?). When you have dinner with friends, your eyes drift toward your phone every thirty seconds. Your fingers are always ready to spring into action and type a response to your clients. You want to do everything instantaneously and perfectly. You realize, to your horror, that you're putting more pressure on yourself than any boss has. You want everyone to love your brand, so you write essay-length responses to every online comment about your product. You spend your nights in Instagram's warm embrace, counting likes instead of counting sheep.

Your search for funding consumes you. When your friends notice that your eyes look a little red, you say it's because of all the adrenaline rushing through your veins. Your Sunday mornings, which used to be so peaceful, are now scheduled down to the minute. You have endless conference calls with your foreign investors. They go on and on about the global economy while your mind wanders. You miss the days when the word "market" meant a stall with nicely arranged cabbages and carrots. You still sing the praises of working without a dress code, but now you hardly have time to take care of basic hygiene, let alone wear your favorite clothes.

You feel like your self-imposed contract has locked you into twenty-four-hour workdays, seven days a week, with lots of clauses about disasters and disappointments. In your whirlwind of raising awareness and building your numbers, you think it's normal to see holidays as a chance to get ahead on your accounting. Your version of pillow talk has become discussing how well your company is doing. You constantly feel frazzled and overwhelmed. But it's only when you find yourself explaining to your next-door neighbor that vacations are for losers with no ambition that you realize you really need to take a step back. You've gone from being a hip entrepreneur to a control freak and a zombie. You can't even blame your lifestyle on a crazy boss—you are the crazy boss. Creating something new is fun, but watching your life fall apart is not. You're exhausted. You dream about the free coffee at your old office, the rhythm of putting on a jacket in the morning and going home at the same time every day. Time has had its way with you, and you're running on empty. You're in desperate need of a pep talk about the benefits of independence, because otherwise you're going to burn all of your business cards and start looking for a job on LinkedIn.

What Would Bergson Have to Say About All of This?

Henri Bergson was a proper gentleman—definitely too proper to ever take part in casual Fridays. However, like Marcel Proust (who happened to be his cousin by marriage), he loved thinking about time. And if there's one thing you need right now, it's time. You can't rush the creative process. You have to be patient. You need to find a way to get that spark back, to take pride in everything you've already achieved. You've lost your confidence, and you've lost sight of why you set out to do this whole thing. You're feeling so drained, not just because of your workload but because you aren't finding joy and excitement in your work anymore. You're getting bogged down in the hundreds of boring day-to-day tasks. You feel like a completely different person from the glamorous, fearless entrepreneur you envisioned at the start. But don't worry. All hope is not lost. Bergson is going to help you get back on track—and chill out a bit.

First, Bergson will help you think about the concept of

effort. Anyone who has ever truly succeeded has put in a lot of effort. Effort is what transforms a beginner into an expert. This effort means trying, failing, and trying again. Bergson says it outright: work is often hard and draining. Though this might sound depressing at first, Bergson doesn't see it that way at all. In fact, he sees effort as an extremely valuable part of life. Knowing that you put in effort is more powerful than success, compliments, or congratulations. This is because hard work makes you a better version of yourself, one with more strength and ingenuity than you ever suspected you had. All of this amazing growth and self-discovery would be impossible without a few missteps. Leaving your professional comfort zone doesn't mean your work will always be thrilling, but life is about more than just having a good time. It's about finding the strength to keep going, even when it seems risky or hard. If you're willing to weather some storms and spend some sleepless nights with your eyes glued to a computer screen, you'll be okay. At the end of the day, even if you miss getting paid vacation, if you stick it out, you'll feel an amazing sense of accomplishment.

Bergson isn't just a philosopher for start-up founders. He can help anyone see the positive in every obstacle in their path. No matter what you're trying to tackle, Bergson will always be there to remind you not to give up on a dream just because you have to fill out some annoying paperwork.

At the end of his writings about effort, he also talks about the importance of creation. Solving problems for your boss is much less satisfying than solving them for yourself. Long story short, you will feel happier about your successes when you have worked hard for them. You will be like an artist who has finished a huge painting, a parent who has raised a child, or a philosopher who has finally determined the meaning of life. The joy that comes from building a business isn't directly correlated to money or fame. Of course you want those things, but the thrill of knowing that you have built something from nothing is even more meaningful.

This, according to Bergson, is the most powerful way you can spend your life: using creativity to make the nonexistent exist. While you're working your tail off, you're growing as a person. While you're building a business, you're also building your character. You're creating something new and entirely your own. Sure, you're working sixteen hours a day every day. You have bags under your eyes, no savings, and no vacation. You've dealt with plenty of failures and will deal with plenty more. But you're growing. Be patient...and the next time you're craving that corporate cup of coffee, make some for yourself at home. It will most certainly taste better, and as a bonus, there will be no one there to judge you for how much vanilla creamer you put in.

Bergson at a Glance (1859–1941)

Henri Bergson was born in Paris in 1859 to Polish Jewish parents. He grew up in London, where he learned perfect English, and in Paris, where he was a brilliant student and won first place in a national mathematics contest. But he was too enthralled by the social sciences to stick with just numbers. He began studying at the École Normale Supérieure at the same time as sociologist Émile Durkheim and leftist politician Jean Jaurès. He earned a degree in philosophy and taught at high schools in many French cities. Thanks to his mastery of English, he also became friends with the American philosopher William James. He specialized in theories of time and consciousness, as well as the difference between intuition and intelligence. He was elected to the Académie des Sciences Morales et Politiques, ensuring that his ideas would influence philosophical study for years to come—and they have, all around the world.

The Book You Need in a Crisis:
Mind-Energy: Lectures and Essays

Throughout *Mind-Energy,* a collection of Bergson's writings and lectures, published in 1919, he argues that philosophy is at heart an instrument of progress. Using scientific data, he demonstrates how philosophy can be a tool for creation and a road to a better life.

Philosophy to the Rescue

- Though it can be grueling, putting effort into your endeavors will bring you joy and help you grow as a person.
- The point of life is to create. Any effort is worth it if it results in creating something new.
- When you work hard, you reveal new parts of yourself, which helps you achieve happiness and satisfaction.

Wittgenstein, Your Boyfriend's Family, and You

Or, Integrating into a New Culture

*Y*ou've never met your boyfriend's family, but you just know you're going to adore them. Hating the in-laws is such a cliché, one that you will never succumb to. You are deeply in love with your boyfriend. You want to learn about and appreciate every part of his life. So naturally you're over the moon when he invites you to have lunch with his parents and siblings. You know you're going to have a great time and that this will be an important, beautiful step in your relationship.

A few days before the lunch, you aren't nervous at all, but your boyfriend is freaking out on your behalf. He's clearly anxious about this impending collision of worlds, and he keeps giving you tips on how to act to make it go as smoothly as possible. You smile and nod, but you don't really listen to the advice. You know you've got this. Ever

141

since elementary school you've been told you have good social skills. You're polite and charismatic, and you truly care about other people. You're going to charm this family. You can't imagine what could possibly go wrong.

The big day arrives, and you're feeling bubbly and excited. You can't wait to look at your boyfriend's baby pictures and hear embarrassing stories from his high school days. But you're running late. You stopped to buy a sumptuous bouquet of flowers, which took longer than you expected. You pull up to the house and everyone is already there. As you ring the doorbell, bouquet in hand, the magnitude of your faux pas hits you like a ton of bricks: you suddenly remember something your boyfriend said about his sister's kid having a terrible allergy to pollen. The door opens and everyone stares at the flowers. You feel awful. You would willingly eat the whole bouquet to make it disappear. Your boyfriend shakes his head, visibly thinking, *I warned you,* as you hear a kid sneezing. Thankfully, your boyfriend's mom grabs the flowers and throws them in the trash. Trying to stay calm, you walk toward the table. Time for a fresh start.

You sit down in a chair, not realizing you're sitting in your boyfriend's brother's spot—where he's sat for every meal since they were kids. You couldn't possibly have known there was a secret seating chart, but the rest of the family acts like it's the most obvious thing in the world. "It's just always been his chair, you know?" they say, seeming annoyed at you. You're paralyzed. It feels like whatever you do you do it wrong. You try to follow the conversation, but it's like they're speaking a different language. Your boyfriend asks his family questions about people you've never heard of. He's so enthusiastic about these people's lives, acting like he's fascinated that X had a baby and Y went to Thailand on vacation and Z got a new job. You feel so uncomfortable. You don't know how to interpret the grandmother's weird hand gestures—is she having a stroke or asking you to pass her another serving of lamb? Lost in the middle of this strange universe, you feel like you're from another planet. Everything sounds like gibberish, and nobody takes the time to add subtitles for you. They keep laughing at inside jokes and old memories. You keep trying to follow the conversation, but they're talking too fast. You don't say anything, and your boyfriend pays no attention to you. You feel like a stowaway on the ship of your boyfriend's life. Nobody has any idea that you're there.

This family is so very different from yours. You were prepared to be open-minded and flexible, but not *this* flexible. During dessert, you have to bite your tongue while your boyfriend's father blathers on about his political views, which are diametrically opposed to yours. Your boyfriend's cousin serves you a piece of cake with a side of self-absorption and arrogance as he brags to you about his job in finance and all of the huge deals he's working on. You try to smile and nod, but you know you're not fooling anyone.

Finally, lunch is over. By the door, you go to hug your boyfriend's mom and she opts for a handshake, as if it wasn't already clear that you're not a part of this family. She gives her darling son a big kiss and a long, drawn-out hug. Then she gives him a knowing look and says that in this life most things don't last, but family is forever.

You get home and you're exhausted. You have never in your life felt so incompatible with a group of people. The confidence you had this morning has been replaced by despair. The idea that you will have to spend sixty more years going to those lunches if you stay with this guy is terrifying. Only a few hours ago you were so excited to look at old photo albums with his parents, and now you're ready for divorce—and you aren't even married! Maybe if you're lucky his parents won't live very long. Or maybe you could kidnap him and move halfway across the world from them. But, realistically, neither of those plans will work. You need to find some way to communicate with and understand this family.

What Would Wittgenstein Have to Say About All of This?

Ludwig Wittgenstein was an expert in the philosophy of language. He also spent time in tons of different places, experiencing many different cultures. He definitely knew the feeling of smiling and nodding through a conversation while actually being completely lost. He channeled all of those awkward cultural missteps into some of his most important works. Wittgenstein has some easy and effective dos and don'ts that will help you integrate into even the weirdest, most difficult-to-understand situations.

In his book *Philosophical Investigations,* the Austrian philosopher explores the link between culture and language. He explains that if you feel lost and can't make sense out of another culture, it's because you can't get a hold on the words and the gestures of the people around you. According to Wittgenstein, what distinguishes one culture from another is not necessarily clothing or folk art or food. Before anything else, it's language—words and gestures, which have evolved according to a culture's history and habits. Every cultural environment uses a different language, with its own quirks. And another crucial thing: different cultures, according to Wittgenstein, are split up not by geographic borders but by "forms of life." This phrase was super important to Wittgenstein. He defined a form of life as a human organization with a specific structure and a specific set of rules. From this point of view, every family is a form of life like no other.

Your world is made up of many constantly evolving forms of life, and you must navigate them every day. Each time you encounter a form of life, even one you're familiar with, you have to relearn its language. If you don't, you risk staying on the outside, unable to communicate, unable to tell if someone is asking you to pass the lamb or is having a stroke. It's impossible to use a language outside its particular form of life. If a form of life changes, the language that goes with it changes too. The meanings of words and gestures vary greatly across different forms of life. At a casual restaurant you can sit down wherever there is an open seat, but you can't do the same when you're visiting someone's family and everyone has a special spot at the table.

When you meet your partner's family, you're crossing a border and entering a brand-new form of life. No matter how good your manners are, this family isn't yours, so there is no way for you to know how everything works. It's the same as when you're hanging out with a new group of friends or when you start a new job. Wittgenstein talks about the necessary learning that takes place as you enter a new culture, calling it a "language game." As with any game, you have to learn the rules before you can join in. This isn't easy, especially when the rules are weird and illogical. To master a language game, you need background knowledge about connections between people, plus an awareness of specific information—for example, you have to learn about your boyfriend's dad's political leanings and that a bouquet of flowers could send his sister's kid to the emergency room. Learning a new language game takes curiosity, time, and care. Above all, you're going to need to accept that your way is not the only way, and you're going to need to know when to sit back and watch. Every group of human beings has its own unique language game. You just have to keep an open mind and patiently learn the rules. Eventually you'll see that if you start to speak their language and respect their rules, your boyfriend's family will come around...and feel better about you playing other kinds of games with their son.

Wittgenstein at a Glance (1889–1951)

Ludwig Wittgenstein was born in 1889 in Vienna, the youngest of eight children in a wealthy manufacturing family. His parents were patrons of celebrated musicians like Brahms and Mahler, and introduced little Ludwig to art and culture early in life. In 1906, Wittgenstein began studying engineering and mathematics in Manchester. He then studied at Cambridge with the philosopher Bertrand Russell. He traveled extensively, especially to Iceland and Norway. In Norway, he built himself a cabin and lived there, because he felt his thoughts were clearer when he was far away from his university. That was where he wrote out all of his thoughts on the foundations of mathematical logic. He fought at the Russian front during World War I, and he wrote his most famous philosophy book, *Tractatus Logico-Philosophicus,* while he was a soldier. The book aims to define the limits of language and philosophy. During the war, Wittgenstein was briefly taken prisoner by the Italians, but he managed to send his manuscript to Bertrand Russell, who got it published in 1922. Since he'd basically solved all of philosophy's major questions, Wittgenstein began looking for something else to do. He became a schoolteacher, a gardener, and an architect, designing a house for his sister. Eventually philosophers in the Vienna Circle started asking him questions and convinced him to get back into philosophy. Then, the University of Cambridge offered him a fellowship in 1939. His research on language and meaning, his thoughts about analytical philosophy, and his eccentric lifestyle make Wittgenstein one of the twentieth century's most memorable thinkers.

The Book You Need in a Crisis: Philosophical Investigations

With a much more approachable title than *Tractatus Logico-Philosophicus*, *Philosophical Investigations* is designed to give the reader a better understanding of language. Wittgenstein walks us through every step of his thought process to help us see exactly how our brains connect words to meaning. The book was published posthumously in 1953 and debunked a lot of common beliefs about the nature of language. *Philosophical Investigations* will help you integrate into new groups and could also save you a lot of money on flowers.

Philosophy to the Rescue

- Culture is, above all else, a language with a specific set of rules.
- Integrating into a group means learning the group's language, which is made up of both words and gestures.
- Cultures are not separated by political borders. Every group of human beings has its own culture and its own unique language.

Thanks a Mill-ion

Or, Treading Carefully Around the Truth

*Y*ou've always loved birthdays—your own birthday in particular. You love being the center of attention and seeing all of your friends show up at a party just for you. As soon as one glorious birthday comes and goes, you start looking forward to the next one. Of course you love seeing your friends on your birthday, but let's be honest: your favorite thing about your birthday is the presents. You're not materialistic, definitely not. It's just that presents are a representation of how much people care about you. You feel like there is love inside every box and gift bag—love in the form of an object that somebody picked out especially for you.

You've been waiting for your birthday party with child-like euphoria. It's your own personal first day of spring. You usually like to open presents as you eat dessert so you can do two of your favorite things at the same time.

The first presents you open are exquisite. Each one of them perfectly reflects an aspect of your personality. You nearly cry as you think about the effort your friends put into choosing these beautiful presents. Your thank-yous and squeals are completely genuine. You're elated. At last, you pick up the gift bag from your best friend, the one who knows all of your deepest, weirdest secrets. You smile a huge smile and reach into the bag and pull out...a sweater? A sweater! The ugliest sweater you've ever seen. You're dumbfounded. Your mouth hangs open. This is definitely the worst gift ever. It's the kind of thing you'd give somebody as a practical joke. It's shaped like a grocery bag, the color makes you sick, and it's made of the itchiest material on earth. What is happening? You look around the room, force your mouth into a smile, and make yourself say, "Oh, you really shouldn't have." The worst thing is that your friend doesn't seem the least bit upset. No, she's grinning and telling you how she spent hours shopping for it, how it's so perfect for you. Unbelievable! The last time you felt this disappointed was when you were seven and your parents ignored several key items on your Christmas list. You feel betrayed. The whole birthday metaphor you've been using is falling apart. If presents measure how much people love you, this sweater means that your friend must hate you. You don't know whether to start weeping or use the candles from your birthday cake to burn your new sweater and rid the world of its ugliness.

Right at that moment, your friend looks you in the eye and asks, "So, do you like it?"

You're no longer the giddy, smiling birthday girl you once were. You have to make a difficult decision. On the one hand, you could lie and pretend to be over the moon about this present that looks like a dirty mop and makes you feel terrible about yourself. On the other hand, you could be honest. You could tell the truth and risk hurting your friend, potentially causing her deep pain and looking like a spoiled brat to boot. The seconds tick past and your smile becomes less and less convincing. Finally you can't bear the awkward silence anymore and you succumb to the social pressure to say something. "Oh my God, I love it," you say. You don't stop there. You keep digging yourself into a deeper hole. "I'm never going to want to take it off," you say. "It's so me!"

The party goes on. Everyone makes toasts about you and hugs you, but all you can think about is the fact that you lied to your best friend—and the fact that you're going to have to wear the ghastly sweater the next time you see her. This is the worst birthday ever.

If you can't tell the truth to your best friend, what does that say about your relationship? Will the friendship ever be the same? Or is it just built on a lie now? If you can't be honest with her about a sweater, maybe you won't be able to be honest with her about other, more serious things. Thinking about losing your friend makes you feel even more sick than you feel when you look at the sweater.

When you get back to your apartment, you think about sending her a text and telling her how disappointed you were with the present. You type out a message, but then, as you're about to hit SEND, you imagine how she'll feel when she reads it. You would really hate to hurt her feelings. That would make things even worse. She truly thought the sweater was a nice, heartfelt gift. So you don't send the message, and you fall asleep feeling confused and guilty. The champagne has worn off, and so has all of your excitement about your birthday. You've started this year of your life with a lie, and you feel awful.

What Would Mill Have to Say About All of This?

John Stuart Mill isn't going to be able to help you make your sweater any less ugly. But the British philosopher and logician can help you understand when it is crucial to tell the truth and when it isn't. Mill's ideas can help you decide when you need to be diplomatic and when you need to be honest in your relationships.

In 1863, in his work *Utilitarianism,* Mill defined the field of economics, the basis of capitalism. He also discussed his ideas about the importance of truth in human relationships. He thought about actions and words in terms of utility, meaning he tried to figure out what would be the most beneficial for the most people. He was adamant about the fact that lies reduce trust. Lying, saying words that are not based in reality, makes all communication between human beings less powerful and less solid. Lying makes relationships between people even more precarious than they already are.

But Mill realized that sometimes telling the truth has serious consequences for social relationships. As he saw it, lying is more than just saying words that aren't true. Lying threatens social well-being. It damages the systems that are set up to make us happy. His goal was to make society happier, and he was convinced that relationships built on mutual trust are necessary to achieve this goal. Telling the truth builds trust, and trust increases human happiness. By this logic, telling the truth is a greater benefit to humanity than lying.

We all know the feeling of relief when we're certain we can completely trust what somebody says. As humans, we have made an implicit pact to be sincere with one another when we interact at work and in our private lives, and that is comforting. In Mill's opinion, if an action will make humanity happier, then that action is moral. Lying breaks down humans' trust in one another, and for that reason it is harmful and immoral. So if telling the truth always guarantees happiness, you can stop there, send that brutally honest text message telling your friend that you hate your present, the sweater from hell.

But even though Mill was a crusader for truth, he acknowledged that, in some rare cases, lying also has its purpose. He laid out several situations in which this is the case, the most important being when lying will protect someone. He thought about extreme scenarios when lying can be permissible. For example, if a criminal is trying to hurt a friend, you can lie about that friend's whereabouts. Sometimes it's also okay to lie to a person who is gravely ill. Looking at it this way, being honest with your friend about feeling disappointed by her birthday present is not a life-or-death emergency. But Mill would also tell you that you have to think about your decisions individually and about how they will affect other people on a case-by-case basis. You can't just look at a list of rules. What will bring about the best, happiest outcome in this situation? Being able to express what you feel, especially if you have been hurt, is essential, on the condition this will not cause someone else even more pain. If telling the truth is going to cause someone else a huge amount of pain, it's probably better to stay quiet.

Almost always, the truth ends up being much more useful than a lie, but there are times when lies are justified. Mill said that if a lie will not only make things more convenient for you but also truly help another person, then it is justified. Worrying about being diplomatic is a form of caring for other people. Lying about everything will harm the precious social fabric that humans work so hard to weave, but lying about a few things is okay. So maybe this time you should put your phone down and keep pretending that you like the gift. You might even learn to love the sweater someday.

Mill at a Glance (1806–1873)

John Stuart Mill was born in London in 1806. His father was an economist who wanted to turn his son into a genius. Mill's father followed the advice of philosopher Jeremy Bentham and gave young Mill a rigorous and strict education. Mill knew the Greek alphabet at age three and began learning algebra, economics, and philosophy at age eight. At twenty, Mill sank into depression and had to regain his balance in life. He finally began paying attention to his emotions after his unconventional childhood. Then he became a journalist for liberal publications. He was a disciple and friend of Auguste Comte, and he supported Comte financially. Mill also believed in positivism, which, contrary to what the word makes it sound like, does not mean he thought life should always be full of positivity. It's just a way of thinking rationally and scientifically. In 1858, Mill moved to a house in France near Avignon. In 1865, he was elected to the British House of Commons, and he advocated for women's emancipation and their right to vote. He admired and adapted Jeremy Bentham's ideas about utilitarianism, believing that when we make decisions, we should always think about the well-being of other people. He focused on the qualitative aspect of happiness. People's main goal, he said, should be to close the gap between their own individual happiness and public, collective happiness. As long as that gap exists, the well-being of others should be more important than personal well-being. His idea of utilitarianism focused on the collective, societal good.

The Book You Need in a Crisis: Utilitarianism

Is it ethical to kill one person to save five? "Obviously!" says the utilitarian in the room. (Everyone else at the party looks a little uncomfortable.) In *Utilitarianism,* published in 1861, John Stuart Mill laid out his definition of the word: the theory that utility is the only way to judge whether or not something is morally right. In this case, "utility" basically means anything that brings the most happiness to the most people. So if wearing an ugly sweater brings happiness to your friend, it's a more useful act than stuffing that sweater in the garbage. As Mill saw it, we're all trying to pursue pleasure in this world—the best act is the one that pleases as many people as possible.

Philosophy to the Rescue

- Usefulness is the best way to measure if an action is moral. Something is useful if it brings the highest possible amount of happiness to society.
- Telling the truth is useful because it builds trust between people. Trust is one of the foundations of happiness in society.
- Lying is harmful to happiness, except in certain cases when a lie is needed to protect someone. It is important to think carefully about your words.

Acknowledgments

Ask me about the story of my life and I
will tell you about the books I have read.
—Osip Mandelstam, summer of 1914

Thank you to my brother, my better half. I owe him everything. If all sisters had brothers like him, the world would be a better place. Thanks to my mom for her steadfast love, her bravery, her imagination, and above all, the bravery of her imagination. Thanks to my dad for wanting this book to be a reality so badly, and for believing in me, which helped me believe in myself. Thanks to Alexandre for being Alexandre, and for giving me shelter when I needed it. This book is ours, and we will remember this for the rest of our lives. Thanks to Coco for fueling me, and to destiny for giving me a third twin and multiplying the love in my world. Thanks to Laura-Maï, for always being there for me as our life paths cross and intertwine. Thanks to Pierre for his lifesaving and indelible writing. Thanks to Sylvie for her kindness and optimism. Thanks to Simon for every month of March together, and helping to melt away the chaos.

I couldn't imagine a more thoughtful, wonderful group of people to help me get through life's twists and turns with a smile.

Thank you to Susanna, Léonard, and Emmanuelle, to whom I am infinitely grateful. Your valuable and insightful editing is more than I could have hoped for, and your faith in me turned me into an author. Thank you to the teachers who made me into a student and the students who made me into a teacher. Every day you teach me to be a little bit better than the day before. Thanks to Alain Granat for showing me that Spinoza is sexy. And thanks to Stéphanie Janicot for the thrill of those first words. Thanks to Bérangère, Carole, Nitha, Rachel, Océane, and Marley. Their enthusiasm and expertise helped me stay sane, and made writing possible. Thanks to Ingrid, an inspired traveler and an inspiring explorer. We'll meet again someday. Thank you to Maud for the elective affinities. Thank you to all the Yiddish moms. Thank you to Virginie, Olga, Jola, Ulysse, Ilona, Malizzia, Eva, and Laurent-David, for the mysterious solidarity and the nourishing encouragement. Thank you to Emmanuel M. and the nights of victory.

Thank you to Spinoza, Aristotle, Nietzsche, Epicurus, Plato, Pascal, Levinas, Heidegger, Kant, Bergson, Wittgenstein, and Mill. When I couldn't figure it out, I asked you guys.

About the Author

Marie Robert holds degrees in French and philosophy. She is a teacher, a Montessori school founder, and the current academic program coordinator for Paris's Lycée International Montessori.

About the Translator

Meg Richardson is currently pursuing an MFA in creative writing and translation from Columbia University. At present she is translating Chilean author Cristóbal Riego's novel *Los pololos de mi mamá* from Spanish to English. Richardson is also writing her own novel, about two thirteen-year-old girls who help their fathers run a pawn shop in the Caribbean. More of her work can be found at meg-richardson.com.